Prince and the Revolution
Purple Rain

Matt Karpe

sonicbondpublishing.com

Sonicbond Publishing Limited
www.sonicbondpublishing.co.uk
Email: info@sonicbondpublishing.co.uk

First Published in the United Kingdom 2024
First Published in the United States 2024

British Library Cataloguing in Publication Data:
A Catalogue record for this book is available from the British Library

ISBN 978-1-78952-322-5

Typeset in ITC Garamond Std & ITC Avant Garde Gothic
Printed and bound in England

Graphic design and typesetting: Full Moon Media

Follow us on social media:
Twitter: https://twitter.com/SonicbondP
Instagram: www.instagram.com/sonicbondpublishing_/
Facebook: www.facebook.com/SonicbondPublishing/

Linktree QR code:

Prince and the Revolution
Purple Rain

Contents

Introduction 5

Purple Rain: The Project..11

Purple Rain (1984)..14

Recording Locations 19

The Album, Track By Track..22

The Purple Rain Tour 47

Reception And Commercial Performance 52

Variations, Reissues And B-Sides...55

The Legacy Of Purple Rain 69

Bibliography 74

Introduction

In the six years leading up to *Purple Rain*, Prince Rogers Nelson had already achieved so much in a career that ebbed and flowed, but to the wider world, it seemed he had barely achieved anything at all.

Born on 7 June 1958 in Minneapolis, Minnesota, to a jazz singer mother and a pianist father, it was perhaps pre-determined that Prince would follow in his parents' musical footsteps. From 12 years old, Prince knew he wanted to pursue a career in music, and boasting youthful exuberance and an infectious effervescence, nothing was going to stop him from realising his dream.

Prince's early musical activity found him playing in cover bands with his friends, some of whom would become professional allies further down the line. Phoenix and Grand Central (later renamed Grand Central Corporation, and then Champagne – sometimes spelt Shampayne) put their own funky spin on songs by the likes of Bobby Womack, Carlos Santana and even the Jackson 5, playing shows around Minnesota for much of the first half of the 1970s. Prince's star power was evident from the start – his funky guitar-playing, mesmerising keyboard flourishes and impassioned vocals quickly revealed him to be one to watch.

His first break came in December 1975, courtesy of Pepé Willie, the then-husband of Prince's cousin Shantel Manderville. Willie formed 94 East – a band named after the Interstate 94 highway, which runs through Minneapolis. The name's significance came from the controversy surrounding the highway's construction, which between 1956 and 1968 decimated the core of the vibrant African-American Saint Paul neighbourhood known as Rondo.

Willie brought a lean and green Prince into his funk band, where Prince played the guitar on all the songs, as well as the drums, keyboards and synthesizers on selected tracks. While Willie maintained the job of songwriter, Prince did get his first co-writer credit on the suave 'Just Another Sucker', recorded in the summer of 1978 at the Sound 80 studio in Minneapolis. 94 East's first collection of songs, *Minneapolis Genius*, wasn't released until 1986, but they largely flew under the radar due to a lack of promotion by the album's distributor, Hot Pink Records. By that time, Prince was one of the biggest artists on the planet, and he had no input whatsoever in *Minneapolis Genius* nor any future 94 East releases. 'Just Another Sucker' is – unsurprisingly – the best-known track of the bunch, but the belated timing of the music's release felt a little too much like a cash-grab attempt from Pepé Willie, using Prince's association as a sales pitch. Regardless of those intentions, Willie is still regarded as the one to first put Minneapolis on notice of Prince Rogers Nelson's talent.

At some point in 1976, Prince and Grand Central recorded a demo at Moon Sound, a homemade studio known to attract young black hopefuls who had a penchant for rhythm and blues. Chris Moon owned the studio, and upon seeing Prince in the flesh, the two struck up a partnership where Prince wrote music to go with Moon's already-written lyrics, and in return, Moon offered Prince unlimited studio time. Within six months of being shown the ins and outs of how a recording studio worked, Prince was running entire sessions by himself: the 18-year-old was impressively able to absorb information and put it into practice in no time at all. With his new skill set came a confidence to aim higher than he thought he was originally capable of – to be able to write, record and produce without any outside interference.

In the meantime, Prince continued to work with Chris Moon, recording demos of songs they wrote together and a few of Prince's own making before he uprooted to New York City to live with his sister Sharon. Taking with him a four-track demo in an attempt to secure some record-label interest, nothing would come of his Big Apple venture despite Moon's own efforts, where, at one point, he pretended to be Stevie Wonder's agent so he could gain phone conversations with label executives.

Prince required a manager, and upon turning down the gig, Moon invited Owen Husney to check out the new kid on the Minneapolis block. Husney was shell-shocked by what he heard. When the budding artist returned home from New York a short time later, Husney met with him. Husney specialised in the promotion of musical artists and, in December 1976, formed the American Artists, Inc. talent agency with his friend Gary Levinson. Impressed by the services Husney was offering, Prince enlisted him as his manager. Next, Prince was flown out to Sausalito, California, for some recording sessions, and some of those tracks made up a demo tape, which was then sent out to a host of major labels.

On 25 June 1977, aged just 19 years old, Prince signed a three-album deal with Warner Bros. Records, having also been courted by other major labels including A&M and CBS. Prince, however, wasn't after a contract where he would be nurtured and micro-managed; in fact, many saw him simply as a singer. But his vision and drive were already well ahead of the curve compared to a lot of artists around, who were richer in both years and experience. Warner knew they had a star on their hands: a raw but multi-faceted musician for whom the saying 'If you want something done right, you've got to do it yourself' was designed. An African American sporting a fancy afro, it would have been easy to stereotype Prince as some kind of soul or R&B singer and nothing more, primed to be manufactured into a pop star to sing pretty and catchy songs perfect for nightclub dance floors the world over, but that was just a tiny smidge of what he was all about.

As his 1978 debut album, *For You*, would quickly reveal, Prince incorporated elements of the above. But he also liked his rock and roll, and funk was what truly set his juices flowing. He also loved to play around with a host of synthesizers, and his experimentation knew no boundaries. Across the 33-minute album, Prince proved himself to be a beguiling figure, on the one hand expressing irresistible affection on the likes of 'In Love' and 'My Love Is Forever', while on the other turning the air sultry with the overly sensual 'Soft And Wet'. The wordcraft and double entendres Prince would become known for can also be credited to Chris Moon, who encouraged his protégé to write in such a way for mass appeal.

Separating Prince from virtually every major label recording artist of the time, his record deal not only allowed him to retain his publishing rights but, more importantly, he was given full creative control of his work. *For You* was entirely produced, arranged and composed by Prince, performing all the instruments you hear on the record, as he would for many of his releases going forward. Prince remains the youngest all-in-one artist to have ever done such a thing in the history of major-label releases, and this was someone who, in 1978, was virtually unknown outside of the state of Minnesota.

'Soft And Wet' was released as a single on Prince's 20th birthday, and the song became a minor hit by creeping inside *Billboard*'s Hot 100 chart at 92. A good result was needed, having exhausted the whole of the three-album budget on bringing *For You* to life, but a lowly 163 peak placing on the Top LPs & Tape (today called the *Billboard* 200) chart left the album's creator somewhat stifled by the lack of reaction. Prince also blamed a lack of promotion by Warner for the slump, and before long, he was delivering a second album to try and reignite his mainstream charge.

More eyes and ears were cast on this bold and enigmatic newcomer this time around – someone housing an incredible vocal range led by a lush falsetto and impassioned shrieks and wails. From the steamy and sauntering 'Baby' to the dreamy acoustic romp of 'Crazy You' – not to mention the dizzying synth-funky 'Why Do You Wanna Treat Me So Bad?' and the riff-tastic 'Bambi' – people really began to sit up and take notice of Prince as the 1970s was set to bow out. The self-titled second effort reached 22 on the US album chart and went platinum within four months of its release, while 'Why You Wanna Treat Me So Bad?' secured a first Hot 100 hit by going to number 11.

A new decade welcomed a new mindset for many, buoyed by conservatism, free-market economics and the advancement of technology, although not everyone so easily embraced such progressions in the world. Prince's third album *Dirty Mind* arrived in October of 1980 and effortlessly revealed an elevation in creativity, which would ultimately set the standard for all of his future work. *Dirty Mind* incorporated new-wave sensibilities into Prince's already-measured funk blueprint, utilising the upgrades of synthesizers and drum machines to create a new musical aesthetic. But it was the album's lyrical content which became more of a lasting talking point over the eight critically acclaimed songs. The incestuous theme of 'Sister' and the obvious connotations of 'Head' were built around complex erotic wordplay, upping the ante on sexually explicit music and opening the door for future artists to follow suit. It was the glorious pop melodies, throbbing rhythms and spongy synths which found Prince to be in a league all of his own; his provocative fusion of styles was hailed by many as setting the scene for the future of urban black music throughout the decade.

Prince had already begun exploring genderfluidity on *Dirty Mind* long before the term became more commonplace in the 1990s before *Controversy* followed in October 1981. The artist already had his fair share of detractors by that point and promptly faced criticism and questions surrounding both his race and his sexuality. Prince responded in the best way he knew: through music. On his fourth LP, he was even bold enough to recite The Lord's Prayer midway through the classic title track, which begins with the lines of 'I just can't believe all the things people say/Am I black or white/Am I straight or gay?'. Backed up by the equally bouncing 'Sexuality' ('Sexuality is all we ever need') and customary gleaming ballads such as 'Do Me Baby', Prince even went political in an open letter to President Reagan, pleading for the end of the Cold War on 'Ronnie, Talk To Russia'. He even touched on the murders of black children in Atlanta between 1979 and 1981 and the assassination of The Beatles' John Lennon on 'Annie Christian'.

Controversy made it to 21 on the *Billboard* 200 and subsequently went platinum, further pushing Prince into America's psyche. But he wasn't quite there yet. Prince was deeply misunderstood, not taken seriously perhaps, and his rise wasn't being helped by Michael Jackson's surge to superstardom on the back of his *Off The Wall* album from 1979 and the upcoming game-changer *Thriller*. Both artists possessed a meticulous songwriting craft based around the bending of genres, and similarities were often drawn between the two, even if their careers would later experience alternate trajectories. Jackson and Prince were pitted against one another in a rivalry created and further amplified by the mainstream media. There would be some minor spats throughout the decade, and one not so minor when Prince was accused of attempting to run down Jackson with his limousine after an impromptu onstage faceoff during a James Brown concert at the New Beverly Cinema in Hollywood on 20 August 1983. Regardless of the hearsay which followed, it was better to let the music do the talking.

On 29 November 1982, Jackson released his sixth album, *Thriller*. An almost perfect record featuring some of the singer's biggest hits, *Thriller* sold over 32,000,000 copies in its first year worldwide. Today it has sold over 70,000,000, and the album will likely forever remain the biggest selling of all time. A month before *Thriller* was unleashed on the world, Prince released his fifth effort *1999*, the first to be recorded with The Revolution. Originally a live band put together by Prince in 1979, having reportedly been influenced by Sly and the Family Stone in enlisting multi-racial male and female musicians, the Revolution was later upgraded to a studio band. There would be multiple lineup changes before settling on the one which would shine so eloquently on *Purple Rain*. The band went unnamed at first, their official unveiling coming on the cover sleeve of *1999*, and the Revolution's arrival coincided with the turn in fortune Prince had been strenuously working towards.

It isn't necessarily the success *1999* earned, as it is the impact which formalised its legacy. At the time, the new millennium was still a long way away, but people had already begun to wonder – and fear – what the implications may be when the year 2000 was welcomed in: if there was even a world still intact when the clock finally struck midnight. Ever the laid-back, live-in-the-now kind of guy, Prince took it all with a pinch of salt and wrote a host of anthems for the public to let their hair down and dance to. He did still find time on the title track to protest against the spread of nuclear weapons and technology, though. The enduring impression of the album found Prince pushing past racial stereotypes by immersing himself into a new scene and picking up a whole new fan base in the process.

The MTV network had launched in 1981 and predominantly catered for rock acts, such was the genre's popularity at the beginning of the decade. Almost all of these acts were made up of white musicians, and within a year of its inception, MTV was being questioned about its apparent racial bias. Even David Bowie was calling them out. By this time, Prince had released the lead single title track from *1999*, with an accompanying music video to boot. After a small mutiny by a handful of MTV employees who pushed for greater diversity in the network's content, Prince started to become featured on the channel for the first time. '1999' received light rotation, but it had at least begun to create a cultural shift. After Michael Jackson's 'Billie Jean' was afforded heavy rotation by MTV in March 1983, Prince's next single 'Little Red Corvette' became the song which saw him cross over into a rock audience. Showing off his pristine guitar skills – where even heavy metal fans were now bobbing their heads to his grooves – Prince was earning greater acknowledgement than ever before.

1999 was Prince's first album to peak inside the Top 10 of the *Billboard* 200. The singles '1999', 'Little Red Corvette' and 'Delirious' all became Hot 100 hits, and the album track 'International Lover' received a Grammy nomination in the Best Male R&B Vocal Performance category. The album itself – with a running time of 70:29 – went on to be certified four times platinum in the US and is considered one of Prince's best pieces of work. This was extremely high praise for the artist, and he would receive even stronger plaudits for what came next. Enter *Purple Rain*.

Purple Rain: The Project

Prince was riding on the crest of a wave in the aftermath of *1999*, and he was now one of the biggest pop stars on the planet. Not one to stick to the same formula that had brought him success, Prince had long been plotting his next move and how he could go bigger and bolder, having captured people's attention. Prince wanted to become a movie star, and he had an idea of how to achieve this in mind.

Having long parted company with Owen Husney, Prince was now part of a stable in which Bob Cavallo, Steve Fargnoli and Joe Ruffalo all managed the artist in one way or another. With their contract coming up for renewal, the trio were given an ultimatum by their client: get him an acting gig, or he would find someone else who could. Upon releasing *Controversy*, Prince had considered creating a movie in the form of a full concert performance whilst incorporating biographical interludes of his life at regular intervals. With the working title of *The Second Coming*, the ideas quickly evolved into a full-blown movie concept. Sleeping on it for a while, Prince put the project back on the table during the *1999* tour, making countless notes for the film he wanted to star in – a semi-autobiographical flick documenting his elevation to becoming the king of First Avenue and then the world. 'I really wanted to chronicle the life I was living at the time', the artist told Larry King in a 1999 interview on CNN, 'which was in an area that had a lot of great talent and a lot of rivalries'.

A precursor to the project came on the *1999* tour, which ran across America from 11 November 1982 to 10 April the following year. Unofficially billed as the Triple Threat Tour – due to its lineup of Prince, The Time and Vanity 6 – the 'triple threat' title came from Hollywood to describe someone who could act, dance and sing. It may have simply been a coincidence, but the Triple Threat Tour would ultimately serve as a prophetic prelude to what Prince would do next.

Bob Cavallo met with a selection of studios to try and sell this brave concept of a musical film. When no one appeared interested, Cavallo decided to produce the thing himself. Cavallo commissioned William Blinn, impressed by his work on the TV show *Fame,* which ran between 1982 and 1987 and followed the lives of students at the New York City High School of Music & Art and Performing Arts, to write the film's script. Blinn would spend hours talking to Prince to formalise a plot based on the musician's upbringing, his music and love. In July 1983, a young and aspiring James Foley was offered the job of directing the film, but he quickly passed and threw it in the lap of his editor, Albert Magnoli. Magnoli immediately scoffed at Blinn's script (titled *Dreams*) which had turned out to be darker than anyone had anticipated. Feeling the script was lacking truth, and in his words being 'very introverted and claustrophobic', Magnoli reeled off his own on-the-spot pitch to Prince, who was astonished to find he had been told his life story in only a matter of minutes, and by a complete stranger nonetheless. Magnoli was hired to direct and edit the film, replacing Blinn.

Warner Bros. took on the picture. However, during the first meeting, Executive Vice President Mark Canton had the audacity to try and get Prince replaced by John Travolta for the lead role. Canton felt Prince wasn't quite the world-renowned figure that his record sales suggested, nor was he a fully-fledged actor who would draw in a strong viewership. Travolta had already shown himself to be rather adept at starring in musical films, as confirmed by the critically acclaimed *Saturday Night Fever* and *Grease*, but it was never on the cards for Prince to be displaced from his own movie.

Warners also suggested *Purple Rain* should be given a PG rating, but Magnoli's vision was leaning towards a Restricted rating. The script also came under scrutiny for its perceived misogyny, eroticism and violence, and it seemed at one point or another that the movie may not ever get off the ground. Magnoli had Michael Ovitz and Mo Ostin on his side, though, one a veteran talent agent and the other a respected record executive. Both of whom just happened to work for Warner Bros. The pair pushed for Magnoli's film to be given the rating he wanted, ironing out any further kinks in the process, and then with a $7,000,000 budget, the green light was given for filming to commence.

If you are reading this book, then it is highly likely you have seen *Purple Rain* – a film starring Prince as The Kid and revolves around the trauma of living in a broken home, fractured relationships, emotional fragility and a love of music where you will do whatever it takes to make your dreams come true. That is the gist of the plot, and the results made for admirable viewing. What should also be mentioned is the cast, most of whom were professional musicians who probably never once considered they would have to do some acting in their lifetime. Morris Day from The Time put on a particularly stellar performance as Prince's rival.

An early spanner was thrown into the works when, out of the blue, the lead actress upped and left. Prince's love interest in *Purple Rain* was set to be his real-life muse Denise 'Vanity' Matthews, who also fronted the all-female trio Vanity 6. During pre-production, Matthews decided to quit her band, her film role and Prince to pursue a career as a solo artist. Auditions were hastily arranged to find a replacement, and out of a reported 700 women to try their hand, it was Patricia Kotero who landed the role. Prince renamed her Apollonia, and she would go on to join remaining Vanity 6 members Brenda Bennett and Susan Moonsie in the newly rechristened Apollonia 6.

Filming began on 1 November 1983, capturing various scenes in and around Minneapolis, including First Avenue (see the Recording Locations section for more information on the venue). Having to stay closed to the public for almost a month due to the frequent shoots, the owners of First Avenue received $100,000 for their hospitality and to make up for the loss of earnings. The entire movie was shot in just 42 days, and its premiere took place at the then-named Mann's Chinese Theater in Hollywood on 26 July 1984. The spectacle was televised on MTV, further showing the network had fully embraced Prince since first putting his '1999' music video into rotation.

Amongst all the acting, filming and everything else going on, Prince was also writing some new songs to be included in the movie and to be released as a soundtrack album instead of a traditional studio release.

Purple Rain (1984)

Tracklisting:
1. Let's Go Crazy
2. Take Me With U
3. The Beautiful Ones
4. Computer Blue
5. Darling Nikki
6. When Doves Cry
7. I Would Die 4 U
8. Baby I'm A Star
9. Purple Rain

Personnel:

Prince: lead vocals, backing vocals, electric and acoustic guitars, synthesizers, electric grand piano, piano, bass, drum machine, drums, tambourine

Wendy Melvoin: electric rhythm guitar (1, 4, 7, 8, 9), backing vocals (1, 4, 7, 8, 9), string conductor (2, 8, 9)

Mark 'Brownmark' Brown: bass (1, 4, 7, 8, 9), backing vocals (1, 4, 9)

Lisa Coleman: synthesizers (1, 4, 7, 8, 9), co-lead vocals (2), backing vocals (1, 2, 4, 7, 8, 9), string arrangement (2, 8, 9), string conductor (2, 8, 9)

Matt 'Dr. Fink' Fink: synthesizers (1, 4, 7, 8), electric grand piano (9), drum machine (7), backing vocals (1, 4, 9)

Robert 'Bobby Z.' Rivkin: drums, drum machine (1, 4, 7, 8, 9), cymbals (1, 4, 7, 8, 9)

Patricia 'Apollonia' Kotero: co-lead and backing vocals (2)

David Coleman: cello (2, 8, 9), finger cymbals (2)

Novi Novog: violin (2, 9), viola (9), electric violin (8)

Suzie Katayama: cello (8, 9)

Jill Jones: co-lead vocals (2), backing vocals (2, 8)

Recorded at: Kiowa Trail Home Studio (Lake Riley, Chanhassen, Minnesota), First Avenue (Minneapolis, Minnesota), The Warehouse (St. Louis Park, Minnesota), Sunset Sound (Hollywood, California), Record Plant Mobile Truck (July 1983-March 1984)

Produced by Prince

Engineered by: David Leonard, Susan Rogers, Peggy McCreary, David Rivkin

Record label: Warner Bros.

Release date: 25 June 1984

Chart positions: US: 1, UK: 7
Running time: 43:51

The recording of *Purple Rain* took place between July 1983 and March 1984. All but one of the nine songs were solely written by Prince. However, the album would be the first to fully credit The Revolution under the 'Produced, arranged, composed and performed by' heading. It seemed Prince had finally learned to play well with others.

By 1984, anyone familiar with Prince was able to recognise his unhealthy obsession with the colour purple. But the mystery surrounding the album and movie title took a while to be revealed. Twelve years prior, the folk-rock band America released their second album *Homecoming* via Warner Bros. Records. The opening song on that album – 'Ventura Highway' – was chosen as the lead single, and it became one of the London-based trio's most popular anthems. Within the lyric – written by Dewey Bunnell – is the section 'Wishin' on a falling star/Waitin' for the early train/Sorry boy, but I've been hit by purple rain'. The band themselves could not provide a specific meaning for the 'purple rain' addition, but it is believed Prince heard the song at some point and liked the term so much that he created a personal attachment to it. After being inundated with questions surrounding his film and album title, he disclosed his perception:

> When there's blood in the sky, red and blue = purple … purple rain pertains to the end of the world and being with the one you love and letting your faith/god guide you through the purple rain.

Far denser than Prince's previous records, *Purple Rain* thrives on its full-band performances and from the multiple layers of instruments which are so innovatively exploited. The music also explores further enhancements of the Minneapolis Sound – the name given to the funk rock subgenre Prince had pioneered in the late 1970s when he first incorporated new wave and synth-pop nuances into some of his songs. Over the years, many critics have described *Purple Rain* as his most pop-orientated album, but it is so much more than that.

With a large proportion of rock fans to cater for after the success of 'Little Red Corvette', the renowned title track presented pure guitar artistry and left new supporters more than content, as did the numerous feisty guitar licks and riffs, which on occasion verged on the metallic. There is, naturally, a profusion of funk running through the heart of each song, while sweaty R&B energy comes from palatial synths to keep original followers engrossed in their idol worship. All convention went out the window on *Purple Rain*, where the painstaking exploration of each instrument emanates the sounds and styles to provide the limitless music you hear across 44 cool and calculated minutes.

Along with a handful of others, Prince primarily used his Hohner Madcat guitar during recording, as he would throughout much of his career. Reportedly costing him just $30 (with one story claiming that it was first purchased at a gas station and another (more likely) stating it was bought from a Minneapolis guitar store), Prince preferred his Madcat when he was holed up in a studio. Debuting the instrument on the *Dirty Mind* tour, its pickups and bridge bore strong similarities to those found on a Fender Stratocaster, thus creating the guitar's unique sound.

The second guitar used during this period was, of course, the custom-made Dave Rusan Cloud, with its iconic spiral shape around the jack and its carved upper horn. Rusan was a more-than-able guitarist himself, and he had previously met Prince when trying out for the live band the artist was putting together after the release of *For You*. Rusan didn't get the position, but a few years later, when he was working at the Knut-Koupee music store in Minneapolis, his and Prince's paths collided once more. One day, Prince came into the store to discuss having a guitar made for a movie he was working on and set to appear in. The job fell into Rusan's lap, with only Prince's Sardonyx bass guitar to go by as some form of template. He was told, however, that the new guitar should have EMG pickups and spades on the fingerboards, and it must be painted white but with small segments in gold. Named after the cloud-designed blue suit Prince wore in the 'Raspberry Beret' music video, the guitar became a legend in its own right, possessing flair worthy of he who would be playing it. Rusan handcrafted the Cloud in a very short space of time. It was, in fact, the very first design that came to fruition, and Prince instantly fell in love with the guitar, so much so that Rusan was later charged with building two more guitars in time for the *Purple Rain* tour.

Wendy Melvoin's Rickenbacker 330s also deserves an honourable mention: the guitar of choice for many rockers during the 1960s. The guitar was modified with Seymour Duncan Hot Stack Tele pickups, a hardtail bridge and sealed-up sound holes; Melvoin was able to reveal a guitar sound closer to Prince's Madcat in comparison to the capabilities of a traditional 330. Her guitars were also refinished in purple.

In the Personnel section a couple of pages back, you will see the number of synthesizers used in the making of the album, and their influence cannot be understated. Here is a small breakdown for those who may be less familiar with how they work. Prince employed a host of analogue and state-of-the-art digital synthesizers, including a handful of Oberheim models. He had used some of them before on albums dating as far back as *Dirty Mind*. The Oberheim OBs are a series of polyphonic analogue subtractive synthesizers which allow multiple notes to be played at the same time, with a method of sound synthesis where small parts of an audio signal are reduced by a filter to alter the colour or quality of a tone being protracted. Also used was an ARP Omni-2, which exports the violin and viola sounds you hear from time to time, courtesy of preset electronically generated orchestral string voices.

A new product in 1983, Prince promptly adhered himself to the Yamaha DX7 – the first truly successful FM synthesizer (frequency modulation synthesis), and one which would become a best seller. Offering a richer and brighter sound in comparison to the fuzzier output of analogue synthesisers, with its preset sounds and five-octave 16-note polyphony, Yamaha licensed the technology developed by John Chowning at Stanford University to create the DX7. Those interested in hearing what it was capable of back then need look no further than the various demonstrations throughout *Purple Rain*.

And then there are the drum machines, the Linn LM-1 being the first to be programmable and the first of its kind to contain samples of acoustic drums. Along with the LM-2 (LinnDrum) which sold many more units than its predecessor and featured higher quality samples, it was Roger Curtis Linn's inventions which helped establish the drum machine as a credible musical tool within the industry.

The first viable electronic replacement for acoustic drums is credited to the Simmons SDS-V, developed by Richard James Burgess and Dave Simmons and commercially released in 1981. With its futuristic-looking hexagonal pads made from the same hard plastic used to forge police riot shields, a lot of drummers intrigued to try out the kits were soon complaining of suffering from sore wrists and elbows. Later versions in the SDS line came better suited to the musician's health by having less robust pads made of rubber, but the changes somewhat lessened the original drum's charm. The SDS-V came loaded with five modules made up of three toms, a bass drum and a snare, while there were also controls for such things as noise, tone level and decay time. Optional cymbal and hi-hat modules were also made available to consumers.

The final configuration of the *Purple Rain* tracklisting was compiled on 14 April, just over two months before the album was released, after plenty of additions, omissions, track edits and running-order changes. The cover art went on to become one of Prince's most recognisable, shot on an exterior set in the backlot of Warners Studios in Burbank, California. Known as Hennesey St. and with buildings designed to resemble a New York apartment complex, the set has been used in other TV shows and movies over the years, such as *Batman* and *Gremlins*. Photographed by Ed Thrasher (who joined Warner Records in 1964 and designed album covers for Jimi Hendrix and Van Morrison, to name just two), *Purple Rain*'s art package was put together under the direction of Laura LiPuma.

With Prince placed front and centre and wearing a rather swanky purple suit, he proudly sits on his Purple Rain Hondamatic CM400A motorcycle. For the movie, the 1981 two-speed automatic model was given a large Windjammer fairing, mini-ape handlebars and a pink velour seat. The motorcycle can also be seen in the movie's sequel *Graffiti Bridge*, for which it was repainted black and gold. Also, on the front cover, Apollonia can be seen standing on a balcony by an illuminated fire escape, staring down at her love interest. The main image is bordered left and right by a floral design, which also makes up the rear cover. Along with the tracklist – where each song title is highlighted by different but effective fonts, there is a poem filling the centre of the rear sleeve. Beginning with the opening line of 'When Doves Cry', the piece quickly evolves into what can best be described as disorientating ramblings surrounding a lover Prince is pursuing.

Although *Purple Rain* contains Prince's signature sound, the album also treads new territory, shattering glass ceilings and investigating previously unauthorised realms: a catalyst for all his future work. It is the album against which his entire discography remains measured – whether fairly or unfairly. And while most artists would happily lay claim to creating *one* magnum opus in an entire career, for Prince, *Purple Rain* is one of many. A nine-track documentary of his life, referencing the grief and despair of lost loves and regrets of missed opportunities, *Purple Rain* is wholesome, reflective and emotionally fraught. Without those feelings, the album would not have powered its creator towards icon status.

Recording Locations

Kiowa Trail Home Studio

Prince moved into the two-story, ranch-style split house in either late 1980 or early 1981, becoming known as the Purple House after the artist completely replaced the original cream paint scheme with his favourite colour.

Located at 9401 Kiowa Trail in Lake Riley, Minnesota, and just a couple of miles from Chanhassen, Prince set up a studio in the former family room on the ground floor. Bringing with him his 16-track recording unit from his previous North Arm Drive home studio, he then purchased and installed an Ampex MM1200 24-track recorder with a Soundcraft 3B console in May 1982. The fully established control room also housed an array of big speakers, while the smaller recording units resembled booths. With little room for it but so he could still record himself when playing, Prince set up his acoustic Yamaha piano in an upstairs living room, wiring it into the studio directly beneath it. Before *Purple Rain*, parts of *Controversy* and *1999* were recorded at Kiowa Trail, as was material by the Time, Vanity 6 and, later, Apollonia 6.

The Warehouse

More commonly known as St. Louis Park Warehouse at 6651 Highway 7, and some eight miles outside of Minneapolis, the setting had previously been used to manufacture farm equipment and had been a metal stamping plant and a pet-food storage facility. A million miles away from being a professional recording studio, the building certainly wasn't there to serve as such, with thick cement walls and poor insulation. Initially rented as a space for band rehearsals, The Warehouse was also used for dance and acting classes for Prince, The Revolution, The Time and Vanity 6, ahead of filming the *Purple Rain* movie. When Prince decided to do some recording there, the open plan meant mics and further equipment were set up right in front of a newly purchased API/DeMedio console, and the music was captured on a MARA MCI JH24 24-track/2-inch tape machine.

First Avenue

Prince made First Avenue his second home in the early 1980s, whether it be for rehearsals or performing to live audiences. His first official concert at the venue took place on 9 March 1981. Its address is 701 N 1st Avenue in downtown Minneapolis; the distinctive curved black building first opened as a Greyhound bus depot in 1937. With its spectacular art-deco style and offering modern luxuries for its time, such as public phones, air conditioning and public showers, the depot was one of America's finest until Greyhound decided to relocate in 1968. On 3 April 1970, Allan Fingerhut officially opened The Depot: the only venue downtown which showcased rock music while also being able to serve alcohol. In a decade when disco music would soon take over, The Depot held its own and hosted Frank Zappa, Ike & Tina Turner, Iggy and The Stooges, The Kinks and The Ramones, to name just a few, throughout the 1970s.

New ownership meant a change in name in 1980 – Uncle Sam's – before First Avenue opened on New Year's Eve 1981. Some of Prince's performances took place in the smaller 7th St. Entry, formerly a dining area attached to First Avenue and specifically opened as a way to showcase local artists. But it was the 1200-capacity First Avenue where Prince thrived, as would the venue itself when the *Purple Rain* project came to fruition.

Sunset Sound
Just a stone's throw from the Hollywood Walk of Fame, the three-studio Sunset Sound was originally conceived by Walt Disney's Director of Recording Tutti Camarata. In 1958, Camarata took a host of commercial and residential buildings and put the studio in motion, where early Disney films such as *Mary Poppins* and *101 Dalmatians* had their audio recorded. Known for its customised consoles, discrete-component equipment and vintage microphones, Sunset Sound – located at 6650 Sunset Boulevard – has welcomed a who's-who of music royalty, from The Doors, Bob Dylan and Led Zeppelin, to The Beach Boys, The Rolling Stones and Neil Young, and Prince, of course, who made studio 3 his primary location between 1981 and 1987. (He did use the other two studios for session work from time to time). *Controversy* was his first album to be partly recorded at Sunset, as was the following *1999*.

Record Plant Mobile Truck
Record Plant was a chain of three studios offering artists relaxed and comfortable environments to work in. The recording industry was to be remoulded because of the less formal approach of Record Plant, and their studios became many a musician's first choice to lay down their new material.

The first branch was opened in New York City in March 1968. Jimi Hendrix was the first to try out the studio on 321 W 44th Street, recording his classic third album (and the last before his passing) *Electric Ladyland*. On 8 December 1980, John Lennon spent the last night of his life recording at Record Plant when, upon returning to his Manhattan apartment, he was gunned down by the deranged Mark David Chapman. Just six hours earlier, the former Beatle had signed Chapman's copy of *Double Fantasy*: the fifth album released by Lennon and his wife, Yoko Ono.

A second Record Plant studio opened in Los Angeles in December 1969, at 1032 N. Sycamore Avenue, to serve artists on the West Coast. Three years later, a third studio at 2200 Bridgeway in Sausalito (ten miles from San Francisco) saw the company expanding further. It was here that Prince recorded *For You*, spending three months at the studio and blowing his whole three-album budget on making his debut release as extravagant as he could.

Also providing mobile trucks under the Record Plant Remote branding, Prince would twice rent them during the *Purple Rain* cycle. The first of which will be discussed in due course, while the second rental was on Christmas Eve of 1984 when the truck was parked outside the Saint Paul Civic Center Arena. After Prince's live show that night, he set straight to work on recording parts of what would be his next studio album, *Around The World In A Day*. He would later move the truck into his Kiowa Trail driveway to continue work on the record.

Today, only the L.A. studio remains in operation, although it has been under new ownership since 2016. The New York chain closed down in 1987, and Sausalito followed suit in 2008.

The Album, Track By Track
'Let's Go Crazy' (Prince)

Purple Rain begins with one of Prince's most defining intros of any song in his entire discography: the happy-go-lucky 'Let's Go Crazy' finding its creator taking a giant leap of faith.

Raised from a young age as a Seventh-day Adventist, which has a theology that runs along the same lines as Evangelism, Prince has never been one to have his beliefs suppressed. In 2003, he became a Jehovah's Witness and was baptised as such. But in 1984, talking about God wasn't going to get your songs played on mainstream radio. Enter 'Let's Go Crazy'. In a 1997 interview, Prince discussed the song and the risk surrounding its content:

> As I wrote it, 'Let's Go Crazy' was about God and the de-elevation of sin. But the problem was that religion as a subject is taboo in pop music. People think that the records they release have got to be hip, but what I need to do is tell the truth.

Despite the song's message of relying on God to guide you through life and shunning the *de-elevator* that is Satan, Prince chose not to name either of the adversaries, so as to avoid radio rebuff.

'Dearly beloved, we are gathered here today to get through this thing called life', announces a eulogising Prince upon the song's opening spoken-word foray, its intrigue heightened by a pensive funeral-like organ. It was a surprising way to start the album – with lyrics subtly floating around religion – but before long, the depth of the theme is replaced by scintillating instrumentation and the emergence of a classic dance-floor rocker.

A basic demo of 'Let's Go Crazy' was laid down at Kiowa Trail on 18 May 1983. Before an official studio take had been conceived, the track was performed and recorded live during Prince's First Avenue concert on 3 August, which was put together to raise money for the Minnesota Dance Theatre. The company's artistic director, Loyce Houlton, personally approached Prince, describing the MDT as being 'financially beleaguered', and asked Prince if he could help by putting on a benefit show. Approximately 1,200 people attended the concert, paying an inflated $25 per ticket instead of the usual $5 entry fee back then, while a further 250 people obtained free entry via either setlists or because of who they knew. $23,000 was raised for the dance company that night, thus achieving their target and then some.

Bobby Z.'s brother David recorded the entire 75-minute performance from a rented Record Plant mobile truck. Mics were routed to the truck with 24 inputs while being split with the venue so engineers both inside and out could mix the sound evenly. 'There really wasn't anybody in the Midwest with a superior truck like that', David Rivkin was quoted as saying during a feature by *thecurrent.org* in August 2016. 'Those guys were all really top pros, and it was wonderful to see and work with them, and I learned a lot'.

The show was the first to feature Wendy Melvoin in the Revolution's lineup. Dez Dickerson had left the band at the conclusion of the *1999* tour, having been by Prince's side since 1979. When Melvoin came in to replace him, the 18-year-old made an immediate impact as she confidently strutted her stuff and rocked out with her Rickenbacker guitar, leaving her accepting audience more than impressed by what she brought to the Revolution.

Tracking of 'Let's Go Crazy' took place four days later at the Warehouse in St. Louis Park, where David Leonard flew in to assist Susan Rogers in installing a new recording console. While the location was never considered suitable to house a fully functioning studio, the expansive and echoed space did at least offer an honest live-sound feel. The vocal tracks and a handful of overdubs were recorded with the console being placed directly in front of the band's rehearsal spot, as Rogers excelled in capturing the strong 'studio' version, which was chosen to open *Purple Rain*. Her career as a recording engineer had now truly begun.

The song sets the tone for what else is to come on *Purple Rain*, with The Revolution making a strong opening statement. Melvoin's abrasive guitar riff takes over from the organ, swooning in and out as it competes with Lisa Coleman and Dr. Fink's sweeping synth patterns and Bobby Z.'s punchy beats. A guitar had never sounded so heavy on a Prince song, while the classic Minneapolis sound was still able to make its mark throughout by way of an irresistible hook. The stellar guitar work conscientiously builds towards Prince taking the crowning glory, his blissful solo squealing and gyrating as the song reaches its breathless peak. Everything about 'Let's Go Crazy' felt different to all which came before it, whereas today, even the game-changing *1999* album feels a little like an overture to Prince's true calling.

With a 4:39 running time, the album version was dramatically cut from the original incarnation, which featured an extended instrumental section made up of further riffs, a piano solo and some samples. As with some other songs to come, 'Let's Go Crazy' had to be edited down to make room for the inclusion of 'Take Me With U', although the 7:35 'Special Dance Mix' was used in the movie.

Becoming a shoo-in on future concert setlists and the opening song on every date of the *Purple Rain* tour, 'Let's Go Crazy' was the second single to be taken from the album. Released on 18 July 1984, the song followed in the footsteps of 'When Doves Cry' by going straight to number one on the *Billboard* Hot 100. It also topped the Hot R&B/Hip-Hop Songs and Hot Dance Club Play charts. In the UK, it was released as a double A-side with 'Take Me With U', peaking at seven. Within four months of its release in America, 'Let's Go Crazy' was certified gold for shifting 1,000,000 copies, this coming before the RIAA moved their goalposts and began issuing gold status for 500,000 sales and platinum for 1,000,000.

During the intro, the line "cause in this life, things are much harder than in the afterworld' appeared a little unsettling upon first listen, but the incessant and infectious rhythm soon wipes away any fears of the afterlife. With its distinctive drum-machine pattern, whirring synths and the toing and froing of the chomping guitars, 'Let's Go Crazy' includes parts of Prince's past exploits while also offering some new accents.

In the liner notes of the expanded 2017 reissue of *Purple Rain*, members of The Revolution shared their thoughts on each of the album's songs. When focusing on 'Let's Go Crazy', Wendy Melvoin spoke of how Prince wanted to tread new ground with his songwriting:

> Pure pop rock! Prince felt confident enough at this point in his career, knowing that he would and could seal his rightful place in Middle America with this song. It lacked self-consciousness. There was no fear of alienating his funk/soul audience. Just straight-up energy and distortion.

Presenting a broad soundscape unlike anything he had come out with before, this is just the first example of Prince's elevation in songwriting craft come 1983. People are still dancing to 'Let's Go Crazy' today, some 40 years later, whether they found the mysterious purple banana or not.

'Take Me With U' (Prince)
During the final knockings of the movie's editing, Albert Magnoli asked Prince to go back into the studio and write one last song: a

romantic duet in which Apollonia could be involved.'Take Me With U' was therefore purposely written for the *Purple Rain* film, used to accompany a series of images showing The Kid and his love interest riding around on his Hondamatic motorcycle. Despite the ups and downs of their relationship depicted throughout, their happy ending was solidified by this pure pop delight, which features the adoring chorus lines 'I don't care where we go/I don't care what we do/I don't care pretty baby/Just take me with you'.

The song's tracking took place on 27 January 1984 at Sunset Sound in Los Angeles. The vocal overdubs took over seven hours to be added, and on 31 January, the final mix was completed after five hours of hard graft. There were minor delays stemming from recording Apollonia's vocals simply because she wasn't a particularly good singer. Prince coached Apollonia through every one of her lines before Lisa Goleman and Jill Jones teamed up to provide a ghost track to make the vocal performance sound better on tape. The duet is a spirited one, though, where the protagonists get into character and go back and forth in professing their love for one another; a sweet and innocent love-conquers-all ballad made up of sumptuous melodies, and, for the first time, a string arrangement.

Leading with a rare drum intro comprised of overdubbed toms and finger cymbals discharging unique psychedelic chimes, these would offer a tiny hint of the direction Prince would go on his next album *Around The World In A Day*. But it is the affluent string section which found Prince widening his musical palate on this occasion. Growing closer to Wendy Melvoin and Lisa Coleman, and seeing them as his most trusted advisors, Prince was introduced to a number of classical composers, and he felt inspired to incorporate such sounds into some of his new songs. For a long time, Prince preferred to work alone. Even upon the arrival of The Revolution, he continued to work by himself, regularly sleeping only three or four hours a night before he was back writing and recording. When The Revolution became a full-time band, there were certain standards and expectations the members had to meet, and once the likes of Wendy and Lisa had proven themselves, Prince began to let his guard down and accept outside ideas and further involvement. For 'Take Me With U', Coleman arranged the strings under Prince's supervision, and she brought in her brother David and friend Novi Novog to perform the cello and violin parts, respectively.

Along with Prince's sparkling keyboard riff and refined synths, the joyous flow of 'Take Me With U' is epitomised by its soaring chorus.

The pop drum fills return later on, and in the 2017 reissue liner notes, Bobby Z. praised Prince's ingenuity on a song he called a 'pop fantasy masterpiece':

> He was always finding new ways to break the mold of how drums were traditionally recorded. If he heard it in his head, he would just play it, no matter if it was what a drummer would actually play or not.

'Take Me With U' was the fifth and final single released from *Purple Rain* – on 25 January 1985, some seven months after the album originally came out. The song reached a respectable 25 on the Hot 100, but the hype surrounding the whole project had begun to subside by this time, and a fifth single did feel a little too much like overkill.

'The Beautiful Ones' (Prince)

One of three songs on *Purple Rain* to be entirely produced, arranged, composed and performed by Prince, and the first to be written for a specific scene in the accompanying movie, the swish ballad of 'The Beautiful Ones' finds its narrator begging his would-be lover to choose him over arch-rival Morris Day. The Kid sings the song directly to Apollonia during The Revolution's latest First Avenue performance while she is being wooed by an infatuated Day.

Tracked and recorded at Sunset Sound on 20 September 1983, the song features one of Prince's greatest vocal performances. His alluring falsetto leads much of the 5:13 running time over a hollow beat, wailing and sometimes spacey synths and a transformative piano pattern. A maturity is evident from the start, as well as a startling honesty in the lyric, where lines such as 'It is him or is it me?' and 'Don't make me waste my time/Don't make me lose my mind' feel far more real and believable than the fictitious film sequence they were written for.

Upon the arrival of 'The Beautiful Ones', the common question circled around its theme and who Prince was calling out. Was it really just playing along to the plot of *Purple Rain*, or was there someone in particular Prince had in mind to declare his love to? One of the contenders was Susannah Melvoin, Wendy's sister, whom Prince had an infatuation for even though she was in a relationship with someone else. Later, Susan Rogers confirmed the likelihood of Susannah being the muse in this instance. Prince shared his own view during an interview with *Ebony* magazine in 2015:

If they look at it, it's very obvious. 'Do you want him or do you want me?' was written for that scene in *Purple Rain* specifically, where Morris would be sitting with Apollonia and there'd be this back and forth.

Although that statement had come straight from the horse's mouth, it would be remiss of us not to consider another obvious possibility. In the early 1980s, Prince formed the female trio Vanity 6. The lineup consisted of Brenda Bennett, Susan Moonsie and Denise Katrina Matthews, aka Vanity. Dating Prince at that time, Matthews' sex-symbol status increased throughout the first half of the decade on the back of Vanity 6's hit song 'Nasty Girl', which was incidentally written and composed by the purple one. The pair's relationship had ended by the time pre-production of the movie got underway, and then Vanity quit her band, as well as giving up her lead role alongside Prince in *Purple Rain*.

Within a couple of years, Matthews had signed a deal with Motown as a solo artist, releasing the albums *Wild Animal* and *Skin On Skin* in 1984 and 1986, respectively. A handful of mainstream movie roles followed as Matthews achieved her ambition of becoming an actress, and then in 1992, she became a born-again Christian. Drugs had played a big role in her life over the years, having suffered physical abuse at the hands of her father when she was younger before she was thrust into the showbiz world by Prince. Reluctantly portraying an overly sexual image, Matthews was seen as the exact opposite of how she wished to project herself: as a clean-cut Diana Ross-like figure who should be judged on talent and not by how she looked.

In 1987, Matthews became engaged to Nikki Sixx, the bassist of hair metal heavyweights Mötley Crüe. Sixx famously overdosed on heroin on 23 December 1987 and was declared dead for two minutes before being revived by two shots of adrenaline. In Sixx's 2008 book *The Heroin Diaries: A Year In The Life Of A Shattered Rock Star*, he spoke of the tumultuous relationship he and Vanity shared and how drugs were never far away from either of them.

Matthews died from kidney failure in February 2016; her years of cocaine addiction are believed to have played a big part in the deterioration of her health. When her death was announced, Prince was in Australia on his first-ever solo tour. During his show in Melbourne, and appearing visibly shaken, Prince dedicated his performance of 'Little Red Corvette' to his former protégé and lover.

Of all the agitated lines in 'The Beautiful Ones', it is the open-ended 'You were so hard to find/The beautiful ones/They hurt you every time', which perhaps offers the strongest hint of Vanity's influence on Prince. The timeline certainly matches up, as her exit would still have been raw at the time of the song's initial creation.

Whether written with Susannah Melvoin or Vanity in mind – or both or neither – 'The Beautiful Ones' is a stunning song in its own right. Prince's emotionally charged falsetto perfectly attributes the first half's warm and soulful instrumentation while continuously distancing itself from ever coming across as cheesy like so many other ballads of the 1980s. And then the onslaught begins, the tension reaching boiling point as Prince lets loose with earth-shattering screams and screeches as he unashamedly declares, 'I want you'. For many a man, desperation feels like a form of weakness, especially when it comes to love, but Prince's direct and emotive honesty exuded through such gut-churning wails makes for the most extreme listening experience. Throw in a fraught guitar piece atop the huge wall of sound created by the dynamic synth patterns: here was a songwriter laying everything on the line.

In 2017, Lisa Coleman described 'The Beautiful Ones' as 'one of the best ballads' while also calling Prince's vocal one of the best 'in history'. Bobby Z. echoed those sentiments by also paying homage to the leader of The Revolution:

It's a shimmering solo performance by Prince, with incredible studio effects on all instruments and his incredible lead vocal. He intentionally left the final scream at the end of the piece, loud in the mix. That scream – the pleading, complete shred of his voice – sent chills up and down our spines the first time we all heard it. And until the end of time, it should do the same for everyone else who listens.

A longer version of 'The Beautiful Ones' exists, but this album cut hangs around long enough to make a lasting impact. The song even dislodged 'Electric Intercourse' from the film and album tracklist due to being far more suitable both emotionally and musically.

It is fitting that Prince's memoir would also take the name of *The Beautiful Ones*, released in 2019 and co-written by US author and advisory editor of *The Paris Review*, Dan Piepenbring. Sadly, the book wasn't completed on Prince's end, his death coming when the project had barely left the ground. It is still a fascinating read, with various insights from Prince as he talks about his younger years, his parents and early portions of his music career. But it is a shame his true vision for the book was never to be fulfilled.

'The Beautiful Ones' the song is a story of unrequited love and hopeless romanticism, and it is brutally intense in its expression. Whether or not it was written with Vanity in mind, there is some heartbreaking poignancy in the fact that the former lovers passed away within just over two months of one another in 2016, and both at the age of 57.

'Computer Blue' (Prince, John L. Nelson, Wendy Melvoin, Lisa Coleman, Matthew Robert Fink)
Computer technology was becoming ever more advanced as the 1980s edged towards its midway point. Steve Jobs and Steve Wozniak had formed Apple just a few years prior, while IBM released the first personal computer – the Acorn – in 1981. And then came the first laptop, launched in the very same year that Prince drew imagistic parallels between lost love and a fear of dehumanisation from dependence on advanced technology. It may have been an inadvertent ploy, but 'Computer Blue' does pose such an association, as Prince reveals his reservations via an explosive funk and punk-tinged electro rocker.

The origins of 'Computer Blue' date back to rehearsals at the Warehouse, where Prince and The Revolution would frequently jam together. Each member contributed parts before they were assembled into some form of a song. However, the first recording of the track was in its live state at the First Avenue benefit concert on 3 August 1983. Five days later, the band started over from scratch and recorded a completely new version at the Warehouse. Fast-forward seven days, and Wendy and Lisa had joined Prince and engineer Peggy McCreary at Sunset Sound. Prince had much bigger plans for 'Computer Blue', so much so that it quickly evolved into a sprawling 14-minute epic. His vision caused more than a few headaches for McCreary, as she indicated in a later interview:

All of a sudden, he wanted to add things like strings, and I said, 'Excuse me, we only have 24 tracks. We don't have enough room'. And he just said, 'Make some more'.

A second Ampex MM-1200 24-track recorder was brought in to almost double the number of tracks Prince could work with. To assist with the increased workload on her end, McCreary called on her fiancé and fellow engineer, David Leonard.

Known as the 'Hallway Speech' version, the original 'Computer Blue' is built around two verses, three equally prosperous guitar solos, and spoken-word passages where Prince tells the story of a man and a woman walking through hallways named after human emotions. Coinciding with the song's lead lyric of 'Where is my love life?/Where can it be?/There must be something wrong with the machinery', Prince appears to revisit a personal conflict surrounding struggles with intimacy and abandonment; the hallways he relates to, lust, fear, hate and pain.

'Computer Blue' was strongly edited down for *Purple Rain* to further make room for the inclusion of 'Take Me With U', although the opening and now famously seductive monologue piece, where Lisa asks Wendy if the water is still warm enough, remains in place. Showcasing a robust keyboard solo and multiple instrumental passages, these parts were also removed from the album version. Losing its darker edge and obvious tonal shifts, the edit may be leaner, but it does sound denser because of the time restrictions the song has to work with.

Prince's often rasping and digitally-enhanced vocal battles with a bruising Bobby Z. drum stomp, obscure synth blasts (including a percussive line taken from the live arrangement of *1999* track 'Automatic') and crushing guitars. Displaying energetic potency, 'Computer Blue' may be the heaviest song of all on *Purple Rain*. This is the only song on the album to have a multiple co-writing credit, where even Prince's father gets an honourable mention. Of the three guitar solos, it is the melodic second which gained the most attention, its origins coming from an old piano instrumental written by John L. Nelson and later titled 'Father's Song'. Beautifully and lyrically played by Prince on guitar and over a synth breakdown, the solo is one of many standout moments on this disjointed but rousing number. In the 2017 reissue liner notes, Brownmark shared his thoughts on 'Computer Blue':

> This is my favourite song on the album. When we first started working on it, it had no bass line – just a synthesizer occupied the bottom notes. Then he had me improvise on the bottom. One day, during a session, he walked over to me and stepped on my fuzz pedal, and that's where that real growling sound came from. He started laughing and hit the floor, yelling, 'That's it!'.

A cerebral track full of swirling synths, eccentric strings and piercing rock guitar, 'Computer Blue' provided further proof of

Prince's meticulous attention to detail. Pop music rarely sounded as ostentatious as this in the 1980s – in fact, comparing it to anything else seems rather futile. In musical terms, the artist was from another planet, and the otherworldly sounds which make up a large proportion of this song could only have been put together by someone as enigmatic as Prince.

Included on the *From The Vault & Previously Unreleased* disc as part of the 2017 deluxe and expanded reissue, a slightly edited 'Hallway Speech' version is the closest most have come to hearing 'Computer Blue' in its intended and extended form.

'Darling Nikki' (Prince)

After such an enthralling and upbeat beginning to *Purple Rain*, no one could have foreseen what was to come next, nor the controversy it would cause. The sexual nature of 'Soft And Wet' and 'Head', for example, were one thing, but 'Darling Nikki', closing the first side of the album, upped the ante in a way certain corners of the mainstream were unprepared for. Prince's rise meant that his every move was now closely scrutinised, and the opening lines of track number five would raise many eyebrows upon first listening.

'Darling Nikki' documents Prince (or the narrator) being seduced by Nikki – a sex fiend whom he meets in a hotel lobby after watching her 'masturbating with a magazine'. A rendezvous follows, where Nikki forces her subject to sign a waiver before entering into a spicy S&M session. A song such as this, from Prince, was unlikely to fly under the radar for too long, even if it was something fans had come to expect from him over the years.

Basic tracking took place at the Kiowa Trail home studio in late July 1983, and this would be the last song Prince worked on with his super tech Don Batts. The duo had shared a fruitful working relationship since the turn of the decade, but Batts was now gone, and it was around this time that Susan Rogers – a certified Prince fan from the beginning – received word that one of her favourite artists was on the hunt for a new audio technician.

Prince preferred to work with women in recording studios, and Rogers was one of only a few female audio techs based in the SoCal area in 1983. While the others were living in L.A. – the proverbial epicentre of the music business on the West Coast – Rogers was willing to go the extra mile and relocate to Minneapolis if it meant working for the artist she had loved since she first heard 'Soft and Wet'. In the years since, Rogers became a cognitive neuroscientist and professor at the Berklee College of Music, and today, she is the director of the Berklee Music Perception and Cognition Laboratory. In 2022, Rogers released the book *This Is What It Sounds Like: What The Music You Love Says About You*, in which she wrote of becoming *Prince's* engineer and not the technician she thought she was applying for:

> There's a world of difference between an audio tech and a recording engineer. To use an analogy from the movie business, the recording engineer is like the cinematographer, while the audio tech is like the crew person who repairs the camera. But Prince didn't realise – or more likely didn't care – that I had no experience in the art of manipulating sound. He trusted my technical knowledge and – somewhat audaciously – was willing to trust my ability to listen.

'Darling Nikki' was deliberately engineered to give off a raw and live feel, which, if anything, encapsulates the nature of its theme and the character of Nikki. The verses proceed with Prince's storytelling vocal over a heavy and percussive drum thrust. The guitar playfully rallies around the provocative lyric, but it is in the louder refrains and when the tension is lifted that the song realises its true potential. The punchy rockouts come from drums which kick and thrash, synths possessing hot and sweaty excitement, and guitars which riff hard alongside Prince's colossal screams. Standing out from the rest of the tracklist, 'Darling Nikki' may be sparse, unsettlingly and shrill, but it still manages to deliver enough funk to warrant its inclusion.

As the song reaches its climax, the mood turns even more bleak when the sounds of wind, rain and thunderclaps play behind some backwards vocals – known to many as Backmasking, a technique where recorded vocals are intentionally reversed to often reveal a hidden message. The choir-like refrain, in this instance, embraces Prince's religious beliefs with the lines 'Hello, how are you?/Fine, fine, 'cause I know that the lord is coming soon/Coming, coming soon'. At the time, backmasking was seen by some as a way to expose younger listeners to negative messages. In rock music especially – which some have long considered to be the work of the Devil – such messages appeared particularly menacing. For Prince, though, combining sex and theology into this one song was a deliberate ploy, underlining his conflicted personality, even if it risked him coming across as blasphemous.

Prince performed all vocals and instruments himself once again, and The Revolution were left firmly in the dark from their leader's

Right: The iconic *Purple Rain* front cover art. (*Warner Bros.*)

Left: The album's rear artwork, featuring a poem penned by Prince himself. (*Warner Bros.*)

Above: Prince and the Revolution – a musical tour de force. The poster was included with certain releases of the album.

Below: The album quickly and unsurprisingly powered its way to the top of the *Billboard* 200. (*Billboard*)

Billboard 200™

WEEK OF AUGUST 4, 1984

THIS WEEK			AWARD ⓘ	LAST WEEK	PEAK POS.	WKS ON CHART
1		**Purple Rain (Soundt...** Prince And The Revolution	+	**2**	**1**	**4**
2		**Born In The U.S.A.** Bruce Springsteen	+	1	1	7
3		**Sports** Huey Lewis & The News	+	3	1	44
4		**Victory** Jacksons	+	7	4	3
5		**Can't Slow Down** Lionel Richie	+	5	1	39

The "Numbers" on the Minnesota Dance Theatre Benefit with Prince on Wednesday, August 3rd, 1983:

Paid Admissions:

1,200 pre-sale tickets at $25.00 per ticket--------------------$30,000.00
8 tickets at $3.00 at the door (after concert)-----------$ 24.00
$30,024.00

1,208 total paid admissions

Complementary Tickets and Promotional Guest-list:

252 complementary tickets returned (out of 300 distributed)
15 club employees on guest-list
22 Prince frontdoor guest-list
29 Prince backdoor guest-list
14 Allan Fingerhut guest-list
18 club employee guests on guest-list (this includes some media)
4 Minnesota Dance Theatre guest-list
4 media guests on guest-list

358 complementary tickets and Promotional guest-list total

1,566 total number of people

Cost Breakdown Sheet and copies of guest-lists, reciepts, etc. are also enclosed with this package.

Stephen T. McClellan

Stephen T. McClellan

The Committee, Inc • 701 1st Avenue North • Office 338-8388 • Information 332-1775
Mailing Address P.O. Box 3191 Traffic Station, Minneapolis, MN 55403

Above: A receipt from the successful First Avenue benefit concert held on 3 August 1983. (*First Avenue*)

Above: *Purple Rain* featuring Prince, the movie star. (*Warner Bros.*)

Above: The Purple One – as captivating on camera as he was on stage. (*Warner Bros.*)

Below: Patricia 'Apollonia' Kotero – from relative unknown to sex symbol in the space of 111 minutes. (*Warner Bros.*)

Above: Wendy Melvoin – barely out of her teens by this time but already a rock star, and showing off her talents as an actress. (*Warner Bros.*)

Below: A smoking Lisa Coleman – in the same scene, Wendy and Lisa confront The Kid over him not using their songs. (*Warner Bros.*)

Above: Dr. Fink and Bobby Z. – a deadly duo. (*Warner Bros.*)

Below: Whether he was Mark Brown or 'Brownmark', the bassist was always ready to link the harmony and rhythm. (*Warner Bros.*)

Above: Firmly in his element – Prince, the guitar hero. (*Warner Bros.*)

Right: *Live*. The cover art for the legendary concert video, filmed in Syracuse on 30 March 1985. (*Warner Bros.*)

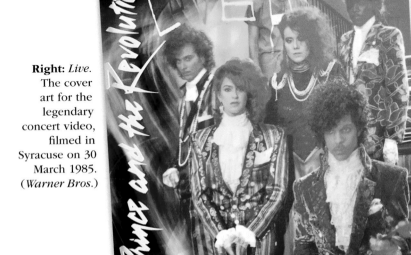

latest composition. A mad scientist concocting a sinister plot and putting it to song, it was only when Prince was happy with the finished article that he shared the results with his bandmates. Lisa Coleman discussed her initial reaction to 'Darling Nikki' in 2017:

Prince recorded this without my knowledge, and when he took me into his car to hear it, it blew my head off musically. I didn't even really register the lyrics because the music was so good! I thought the first verse was just cheeky enough to get attention, and I was excited to play it for all the people who were going to freak out when they heard it, too.

'Darling Nikki' would gain notoriety in the aftermath of the album's release, but it wasn't for its musical prowess. When Tipper Gore – the wife of future Vice President of America Al Gore – bought a copy of *Purple Rain* for her 11-year-old daughter, she couldn't believe what she was hearing when track five kicked in. In her 1987 book *Raising PG Kids In An X-Rated Society*, Gore refused to hide her disgust for the song:

When we brought the album home, put it in our stereo and listened to it together, we heard the words to 'Darling Nikki' ... The vulgar lyrics embarrassed both of us. At first, I was stunned, but then I got mad! Millions of Americans were buying *Purple Rain* with no idea what to expect. Thousands of people were giving the album to their children, many even younger than my daughter.

As the 1980s progressed, artists within the pop and rock genres became more risqué with their lyrical content. Pop and R&B frequently referenced sexual themes, and innuendo was rife. Heavy metal did the same, as well as adding lethal doses of violence and a little bit of Satanism for good measure. Enough was enough for Tipper Gore. In April 1985, she and three friends founded the Parents Music Resource Center (more commonly known as the PMRC) in a bid to increase a parent's control over their children's access to music considered sexual, violent or citing drug use without being given prior warning. All four women were married to men with strong ties to the Washington government, so their protestation for censorship was always going to receive support from those in positions of power.

As part of their campaign, the PMRC presented a list dubbed the Filthy Fifteen: a set of songs the group deemed to be the most offensive. 'Darling Nikki' topped the list. A second song tied to Prince was also on there – 'Sugar Walls', which had been written under his 'Alexander Nevermind' pseudonym and recorded and released by Sheena Easton. Vanity's 'Strap On Robbie Baby' also made the list, as did Mötley Crüe's 'Bastard' from their *Shout At The Devil* album. 'Animal (Fuck Like A Beast)' by W.A.S.P. was another heavy-metal entry. The L.A. quartet's full name has remained shrouded in mystery over the years, if indeed they have one, but on their debut album, they did refer to themselves as 'We Are Sexual Perverts', so make of that what you will.

The PMRC fought the RIAA (Recording Industry Association of America) to create a rating system similar to that of movie-age restrictions. In November 1985, 19 of the biggest record labels agreed to begin putting generic 'Parental Advisory' stickers on albums at their own discretion as a way to warn consumers of what they were about to purchase. For a while, Walmart refused to sell albums possessing the warning, while other stores would only sell such records to adults. 'Darling Nikki' has long been considered the song responsible for the creation of the 'Parental Advisory' label, but for many artists whose albums were forced to adopt the warning, their record sales actually increased because of it.

When performed on the *Purple Rain* tour, the backmasking on 'Darling Nikki' was actually played forwards. For six years in the 2000s, though, the song was cut from Prince's setlists after he became a Jehovah's Witness; its content was a bit too naughty for he who had penned it and the code he was now choosing to live by. In the 2017 liner notes, Bobby Z. perfectly detailed the song's ultimate brilliance:

Another solo effort by Prince that pretty much sums up all the badness, mischief and troublemaker Prince had in him. Rebellious, controversial, sexual, powerful and percussive, 'Darling Nikki' transformed the studio into a cavern of sound. Again, with his blood-curdling screams, he reaches into your soul and pounds you with eroticism, drums, bass, synthesizers and his blazing guitar work. I was in awe on first listen.

'When Doves Cry' (Prince)
The final song to be written and recorded for *Purple Rain*, 'When Doves Cry' would lay the foundations for both the album and the movie to be the successes they were.

Wanting to capture the overwhelming theme of the film in a specific scene and through a single song, Albert Magnoli asked Prince to come up with one more track, and the artist promptly delivered it. Dealing equally with a tempestuous love affair and a deteriorating parental relationship which threatens to impact the actions of their son, 'When Doves Cry' was reportedly inspired by Susan Moonsie, who was romantically involved with Prince on and off between 1980 and 1985. She had previously been the subject of another of Prince's songs, 'Private Joy', which appears on his *Controversy* album. It is believed that Moonsie ended the relationship when Vanity arrived on the scene, but Moonsie didn't flee too far as she would go on to join Vanity 6 upon their formation.

Interestingly, the song and its structure are said to have been influenced by Stevie Nicks' grief-stricken rocker 'Edge Of Seventeen'. Featured on her 1981 album *Bella Donna*, the track found Nicks coming to terms with the deaths of her uncle and John Lennon, who passed away within days of one another in December 1980. During the first half of the 1980s, Prince and Nicks formed a strong friendship despite spending little-to-no time together. Nicks herself had found inspiration in Prince's music, with her 1983 song 'Stand Back', after hearing 'Little Red Corvette' on the radio while she and her new husband Kim Anderson were on the way to their honeymoon suite. Drawn to the song's melody and its use of synthesizers, Nicks spent her first night as a newlywed recording a demo of 'Stand Back'. Though uncredited, Prince played the synths on the studio version, as well as programming the drums when it appeared no one else in Nicks' camp knew how to.

The lyricism of 'When Doves Cry' is stunning at times, with positive aspects of romance portrayed through Prince's poetic wordcraft, such as this vivid second verse passage:

Dream if you can a courtyard
An ocean of violets in bloom
Animals strike curious poses
They feel the heat
The heat between me and you

Possessing one of the strongest choruses of Prince's entire career – both melodic and semi-autobiographical – he follows the subplot of the movie by sharing his fears of following in his parents' footsteps. In certain scenes, The Kid's father is physically abusive towards his son and his wife. The Kid then repeats his father's actions with Apollonia; for some people, the scenes prove uncomfortable to watch because of the apparent misogyny on show. A large proportion of the criticism surrounding the *Purple Rain* flick in the years since surrounds the mistreatment of the female characters, which, unfortunately, was the norm in the socio-political times of the 1980s. There was a clear divide in the equality of men and women back then, and many contemporary reviews of the film made valid points that *Purple Rain* let itself down a little by appearing to simply go with the flow.

It is in the chorus of 'When Doves Cry' where Prince lays it all on the line and exposes his emotional insecurities while also accepting some of the blame for his latest relationship collapse because of his past traumas:

How can you just leave me standing
Alone in a world that's so cold?
Maybe I'm just too demanding
Maybe I'm just like my father, too bold
Maybe I'm just like my mother
She's never satisfied
Why do we scream at each other?
This is what it sounds like when doves cry

The lasting impact of this song comes from its bass-less arrangement. Straying from convention, the stark texture of hyperactive guitar, a combative drum machine rhythm and dazzling synths were all that was required for posterity here – the formula extremely unusual for a pop song of the 1980s. Making full use of the LM-1 drum machine, the ping-pong-like percussive sound came from Prince taking a recording of a snare rimshot and tuning it down an octave before running it through a guitar processor. His versatile knowledge of multiple instruments appeared unrivalled back then, or perhaps that perception was just due to Prince's high-rising status in comparison to other musicians. But, when it came to programming drum machines, Prince was most certainly one of the best in the business.

Prince was cautious of omitting the bass in the beginning. He would play the song recording over and over again in the studio, first with the bass and then without it, and seeking reassurance to proceed with his bold intention, it was Jill Jones who told Prince to go with his gut. Tracking commenced on 1 March 1984 at Sunset Sound with Peggy McCreary at the helm, and four days later, the song was finished. In a later interview, McCreary spoke of how Prince knew from the start that he had created more magic:

> Prince took out the bass and he said, 'There's nobody that's going to have the guts to do this', and he was smiling from ear to ear. He felt this was the best, and he knew he had a hit song … so he decided to do something really daring. That's what Prince was all about.

An octave pedal was used to give the absorbing guitar parts greater depth; a rapid opening solo soon steps aside for riffs and shreds aplenty. As with much of the nearly six-minute running time, the chorus thrills with a hypnotic synth lead and the repetitive but incisive drum rhythm. Later, a classical-like keyboard piece provides further weight before Prince goes into full-blown guitar-hero mode with his electric enthusiasm. Further forceful vocal wails and a haywire synth solo briefly take things in a different direction before the original flow reclaims the lead on an extended playout.

The internet started to break new ground in the 1990s. Websites have become an important tool for all industries, especially for musicians. On one of Prince's first sites, he decided to upload virtual liner notes for some of his songs, and here is his exact entry for 'When Doves Cry':

> Originally recorded with bass, backing 2 sets of keys and guitar. Frustrated with the mix, [Prince Rogers Nelson] sat discouraged in the studio (Sunset Sound). [Former Prince backing vocalist and protégé] Jill Jones came 2 visit, saw the long face and asked what was wrong. PRN was said 2 have said, 'If I had my way the song would sound like this'. He then shoved down the bulk of the instrument faders and left up only the drums and the xylophone, when the voices began to sing the chorus. Jill then asked PRN why he thought he couldn't have his way with the mix. There was no reply. Everyone who passed by the studio was enthralled by the strange sound coming out of Studio 3 that day. The next time Jill heard the song it was on the radio and it was bassless and stark. PRN had his way.

Warner executives were stunned upon first hearing 'When Doves Cry'. It was to be the lead single from *Purple Rain*, but because of its distinctive sound and with such a key component missing from its manifesto, the label was stumped as to how they would market the song. They didn't even think radio stations would take it on. But their cynicism would be shortlived.

'When Doves Cry' was released on 16 May 1984, just over a month before *Purple Rain* and two months before the movie. On 7 July – six weeks after first charting – the song earned Prince his first number one on the Hot 100, where it remained for five consecutive weeks. In the US, it sold over 2,000,000 copies and was therefore certified platinum. Prince would be the last solo artist to receive the certification in its original format when, in 1989, the RIAA realigned single sales requirements to mirror those of albums: 500,000 for gold and 1,000,000 for platinum. In the UK, 'When Doves Cry' peaked at four and went platinum after hitting the country's 600,000 milestone.

'When Doves Cry' will forever be considered one of Prince's greatest songs, and it has been included in 'Best Songs of All Time' lists in revered publications, including *Rolling Stone* and *Spin*. It's a *bona fide* classic and pure pop magic despite its non-traditional songwriting standards.

'I Would Die 4 U' (Prince)

Faith is going to help you in all aspects of life. Once you clean out the cobwebs, so to speak, and then you're going to be able to see things more clearly.
Prince

Returning to the warm-hearted disco-funk style in which Prince had cut his chops since first arriving on the scene, 'I Would Die 4 U' actually dates back to 1982, when early iterations were tried out during soundchecks on the *Controversy* tour. The final version found on *Purple Rain* was another to have been recorded live at the famous First Avenue benefit concert before overdubs were added at Sunset Sound at the end of August, with mixing then completed on 3 September 1983.

While the album version clocks in at a brisk 2:51, a ten-minute extended mix was also recorded and later released in 1989 as a B-side on the Germany exclusive 'Erotic City' Dance Mix CD single. There is also a 31-minute take which comes from a rehearsal jam ahead of the *Purple Rain* tour, but only bootlegged copies of it exist. This elongated but interesting version finds Prince and the Revolution joining forces with Sheila E. and members of her own backing band, who were one of two support acts on the 98-date extravaganza.

By her early 20s, Sheila Cecilia Escovedo had already performed with a host of music greats, such as Marvin Gaye, Lionel Richie, and Diana Ross. In 1977, Sheila joined George Duke's jazz-fusion band. Duke had released eleven albums by this point, and Escovedo would play percussion on his next four LPs – *Don't Let Go* (1978), *Follow The Rainbow* and *Master Of The Game* (1979), and *A Brazilian Love Affair* (1980).

It was sometime around 1977 when Prince first met Sheila, and he soon vowed that one day he would have her join his band. Sheila would prove to be an artist in her own right, though. After providing backing vocals on 'Erotic City' (a *Purple Rain*-era song and B-side of the 'Let's Go Crazy' single), she released her debut solo album under the Sheila E. moniker in 1984 through Warner Bros. Records. *The Glamorous Life* featured plenty of funk and pop-rock delights, and the title track scored a top-ten hit in America, while the album itself reached a high of 28 on the *Billboard* 200. Produced by Prince under another of his pseudonyms – The Starr Company – he would continue to be involved in Sheila E.'s career further into the decade, as would Sheila E. in Prince's, participating in the recording of songs on the *Around The World In A Day*, *Parade*, *Sign O' The Times* and *Lovesexy* albums. The couple also became romantically involved during the middle of the decade, and for a brief period in 1987, they were engaged to be married before going their separate ways after the *Lovesexy* tour.

On the super extended mix of 'I Would Die 4 U', Sheila E. plays live percussion, as the beats heard on the recording could not be replicated outside of a studio. Eddie 'M' Mininfield plays the saxophone and provides a thrilling solo, while Miko Weaver adds further guitar. Originally a 31-minute track, but in this instance trimmed down by two-thirds, the edit at least maintained all the pivotal moments, which made the jam impressionable in the first place, even if it was an extremely time-consuming listen.

The sound of 'I Would Die 4 U' is firmly representative of the 1980s and is built around an insistent rhythm, swelling synths devised with laser precision, and delicious melodies. The song's rhythm was created via the LM-1 drum machine run through guitar effects before being given further flare in the studio. Though musically colourful, Prince's mastery comes in his vocal, as he relays a brilliant lyric stacked with religious references. However, they could also be construed as painting a romantic portrait. The opening passage encapsulates Prince's enigma as he evokes Jesus' message to his followers while likening himself to a modern-day messiah: quite a bold statement. 'I'm not a woman, I'm not a man/I am something that you'll never understand', he sings, seemingly revisiting the *Controversy* era when his sexuality was brought into question.

'Prince told me that his father had said one time, 'I would die for you'', claimed Albert Magnoli, and it is with this kind of loving devotion that the lead lyric is fully embraced, whether it be in the familial or romantic sense. In the film, 'I Would Die 4 U' follows The Revolution's return to form at First Avenue, their spot on the bill at risk but salvaged by the red-hot debut of 'Purple Rain', before this track builds momentum on a blistering encore. Prince's words of self-sacrifice sound even more powerful in the motion picture, considering everything The Kid has been through to get to a point of wider acceptance, much like Prince himself had been through both personally and professionally. The fourth single from the album, 'I Would Die 4 U' was released on 28 November 1984, reaching eight on the Hot 100 and earning gold certification.

A song as entrancing as a roomful of glitter balls, illuminated not just by nightclub spotlights but by Prince's ethereal charm and songwriting genius, after the hard-hitting 'Darling Nikki' and the emotional rollercoaster of 'When Doves Cry', 'I Would Die 4 U' returns to an alternative serenity where love conquers all, as long as you are willing to believe.

'Baby I'm A Star' (Prince)

'I Would Die 4 U' segues straight into 'Baby I'm A Star', maintaining a joyous victory lap where in the movie, the young pretender that is The Kid finally fulfils his potential and rocks a jam-packed First Avenue with a career-catapulting encore.

As a stand-alone song, 'Baby I'm A Star' finds Prince reflecting on his own life-altering moment, initially believed to be his *1999* album, which skyrocketed him into the major leagues of pop. 'Oh baby … I'm a … star/Might not know it now, baby/But I are, I'm a star', he beams with soulful swagger, the lyric slightly self-indulgent but earnest nonetheless.

The third of the three tracks recorded live at First Avenue, overdubs and mixing took place in late August before the song was completed in the second week of September. An earlier studio recording was made sometime in either late December 1981 or early 1982 by Prince alone at Kiowa Trail; therefore, the lyric more likely points to his increased exposure after the release of *Controversy*, when he received his first invitation to perform on *Saturday Night Live*. The show helped numerous artists get their name out to the masses, so this was a big break for Prince. And even though he wasn't the main musical guest on the episode, his performance of the *Dirty Mind* track 'Partyup' went down a storm. *1999* wouldn't be released until October 1982, but somewhere along the line – whether it be a prophecy or an assured confidence in what was to come – Prince knew he was onto something special, and the lyrics of 'Baby I'm A Star' perceive this.

After further use of backmasking in the song's intro – which in this instance seems rather needless ('Like, what the fuck do they know?/All their taste is in their mouth/Really, what the fuck do they know?/Come on baby, let's go crazy!') – 'Baby I'm A Star' reveals itself to be an unashamedly 1980s pop-pomp romp. There is a lot going on here – an emphatic dance anthem where the music underlines the overall mission statement with a forceful looped drum rhythm, layers of shiny synths simulating a horn section, and piano and keys which formalise a bluesy undercurrent. A driving bass groove and raucous guitar parts heighten the euphoria, while Novi Novog's one-take electric violin piece alongside David Coleman and Suzie Katayama's cello additions only increase the song's grandiose and dense presentation. During a brief pause for breath in the middle, Dr. Fink leads with a warm synth solo before a reinvigorated Prince reappears with another fiery solo of his own, courtesy of his raging guitar. Throughout, Wendy and Lisa's backing vocals are some of the best found across the whole album and are at their most accentuated during Prince's 'I'm A Star' deposition.

The urgency in keeping the momentum going cannot be ignored, even though this is the penultimate track on the album. A lot has happened to get to this moment, but whether from a personal standpoint or from the point of view of the movie itself, the positioning of 'Baby I'm A Star' in the tracklist feels like a masterstroke, as it allows the listener one final opportunity to get down and boogie.

In the 2017 reissue liner notes, Bobby Z. wrote:

'Baby I'm A Star' became Prince's declaration of self-stardom. He led the band on this uptempo track with the authority of a ringmaster. Also recorded live at the '83 First Avenue show, the song became a marathon on the tour, with stops, starts and endless horn punches. He was in his element.

As Bobby mentioned, the song indeed became a marathon in the live setting. Prince and The Revolution were joined on stage by Sheila E. and her band, with other guests such as Apollonia 6 and Susannah Melvoin on occasion, and even famous figures who just happened to be in attendance. The original 4:24 mix quickly stretched to ten and then 20 minutes, and as the tour progressed, the song lasted upwards of half an hour. Incorporating cover medleys and a large amount of improvisation, everyone followed Prince's direction as a huge band jam took place in front of thousands of people every night in arenas all across the US.

A song that is still a whole lot of fun, 'Baby I'm A Star' may not reach the same heights as some of the other tracks on *Purple Rain*, but maybe it wasn't supposed to. Instead, it acts as a party piece to salute the changing of the tide, the achievement of a dream realised through hard work and perseverance. 'Baby I'm A Star' is best showcased in the movie, where The Kid realises his time has come and his doubters have been proven wrong. End scene. Credits roll.

The pressures of fame would overwhelm Prince in the years which followed. But in those final scenes on stage at First Avenue with an adoring crowd having the time of their lives, the glint in his eyes and the smile on his face form the most convincing part of the entire motion picture. Prince was now a star beyond any shadow of a doubt.

'Purple Rain' (Prince)

Touring the *1999* album found Prince inadvertently following a similar route around America to Bob Seger, who was on a roll with the Silver Bullet Band and their acclaimed 1982 record *The Distance*. With a number of memorable folk-rock songs under his belt, such as 'Turn The Page', 'Night Moves' and 'Against The Wind', it was the Detroit songwriter's ability to tell relatable stories through his music which enamoured him to audiences far and wide. Attending some of Seger's shows as their tours zig-zagged, Prince saw firsthand the rocker's uncanny ability to connect with a crowd. When Matt Fink implored Prince to write a song in the style of Seger – a song which would allow him to fully crossover into the white demographic – Prince stepped out of his comfort zone and penned a rather uncharacteristic power ballad. It would become the centrepiece of the entire *Purple Rain* project and arguably Prince's most famous song of all time.

The final mix of 'Purple Rain' was a long way from how it first started out: as a country song, nonetheless. Prince's idea was for it to be a duet, and Stevie Nicks was his intended partner in crime. Receiving a ten-minute instrumental and asked to write some lyrics for the composition, the Fleetwood Mac starlet was instantly overwhelmed by the magnitude of the task at hand. Nicks later admitted to *Mojo* that she 'got scared': 'I told him, 'Prince, I've listened to this a hundred times, and I wouldn't know where to start. It's a movie, it's epic".

Prince returned to the drawing board. Writing and rehearsal sessions began at The Warehouse in the early summer of 1983, and it was when Wendy Melvoin proceeded to play those now recognisable opening guitar chords that 'Purple Rain' took on a new lease of life. Out went its overly-country leanings, and after six hours of incessant writing, playing and arranging, the bulk of the song was in place.

In the movie, 'Purple Rain' proves to be The Revolution's saving grace. Threatened with being booted from their regular slot at First Avenue, The Kid is forced to re-evaluate his situation and, for the first time, accept input from his bandmates. For a long time, he refuses to listen to a demo prepared by Wendy and Lisa, and although the song is credited to the duo ahead of its debut performance (and dedicated by The Kid to his father who has just attempted suicide), 'Purple Rain' was all Prince's own work. The parallel, which runs between those scenes and reality, is the audience's reaction – who stare on in amazement at the song's emotional fragility and the instrumentation's continuous build towards a breathtaking crescendo.

Written in the key of B-flat major, 'Purple Rain' was also recorded live at the First Avenue show on 3 August 1983. The audience was left in stunned silence, in awe rather than confusion at the beauty with which the song expressed itself. David Rivkin said in a feature by *Kottke.org* in February 2023:

It was incredible. I mean, little did I know that it was gonna be that big of a recording. Prince was really not a well-known figure back then. This is the kind of recording that launched him into superstardom.

Melvoin's sombre lone guitar sets the tone for what is to come: slow, sauntering and reflective, leading into the first drum sequence. And the stage is set for Prince, who tiptoes in with the pained opening lines 'I never meant to cause you any sorrow/I never meant to cause you any pain', the hairs on the backs of millions of necks promptly standing to attention. A gospel-like Yamaha electric CP80 piano piece provides a darker tone while the sentiment already radiating from the song continues to rise as each minute passes. A simple but effective chorus refrain of the song title tentatively elevates before the flow returns to its initial dream-like state, and by the end of the second verse, the chant of 'Purple Rain' becomes ever-more powerful through the use of backing vocals, which are sung in unison by The Revolution.

Each verse ties nicely into the film, focusing on relationships The Kid encounters on his journey from childish ignorance to empathetic adulthood. It is evident that love and the loss of love are at the forefront, though, and it is widely believed that 'Purple Rain' was written about Denise Matthews. It sounds as if Prince was still coming to terms with her departure at this time, his desolation on full show as his lyrics act as a letter of apology to the one who got away. A fourth verse revolving around money was included in the original and longer version of the song, but Prince felt it would lessen the emotional impact. The verse was rightfully removed during later edits.

Lisa Coleman wrote the melancholic string arrangement, where the violin and cello work wholly embrace the mood already presented to them. As everything reaches its peak, Prince's guitar takes on a life of its own, his most incomparable solo a blissful reprisal in which he plays as if his life depended on it. Escaping the arrangement as Prince works the fretboard with a smooth sophistication, it is no surprise the solo has been widely regarded as one of the greatest in history by multiple esteemed publications, including *Guitarplayer. com* and *Guitarworld.com*.

'Purple Rain' melds various styles, but it predominantly falls into the rock genre, and when the song was completed, Prince was worried it sounded a little too much like Journey's 'Faithfully' from the San Francisco outfit's 1983 album *Frontiers*. The similarities between the two songs come down to the chord changes and the tone of the guitar solos, but it was enough for Prince to feel the need to contact Journey's rhythm guitarist and keyboard player Jonathan Cain. Politely enquiring whether he would be sued by the band if he released 'Purple Rain', Cain jumped to reassure Prince there was no issue to be discussed. 'I thought it was an amazing tune', Cain recalled in a 2016 interview with *Billboard*. 'I just thought it seriously showed the kind of caring, classy guy Prince was'.

While 'Purple Rain' is the out-and-out love ballad it presents itself to be, the lyric also bears religious undertones much like those on 'Let's Go Crazy'. 'You say you want a leader, but you can't seem to make up your mind/I think you better close it and let me guide you through the purple rain', sings Prince as he once again assumes the identity of a messiah. Further emphasising his skill of forming multiple meanings through his words, it was at this moment that the album came full circle.

When the instrumentation comes together for the riveting finale, it is Prince's emotive, high-pitched wails which supply the ultimate parting gift. Over the explosive guitars, the arena-sized drum rhythm and synths and strings aplenty, it is the desperation in Prince's voice which is the most palpable here: the peak moment on a song that is full of outstanding highs. Timeless from the moment it was recorded, 'Purple Rain' still boasts a wealth of vitality some 40 years later. Never sounding outdated like so many songs from the past, and with an alluring presence that still affects and unites us, 'Purple Rain' is the song by which all future power ballads were set to be measured.

Released as the album's third single on 26 September 1984, 'Purple Rain' debuted at 28 on the Hot 100 a week later. The song slowly progressed up the chart before peaking at two on 17 November, where it remained for two weeks and secured gold certification. Denied the top spot by the bubblegum pop of 'Wake Me Up Before You Go-Go' by Wham!, it would've been interesting to see how the track could've fared had it been the lead single instead of 'When Doves Cry', not that the latter failed in any way. 'Purple Rain' did go to number one on US Hot Rock Songs, though, and also on numerous charts throughout Europe, while in the UK, its best position was six, selling 1,200,000 copies and earning double-platinum status.

Many enthusiasts will likely have 'Purple Rain' lower down on their list of favourite Prince cuts, but for a lot of impartial music listeners, the ballad will forever be seen as Prince's defining moment. It is the story of a longing for love while combining feelings of regret, loneliness and desire. Consistently ranked amongst the greatest songs of all time by many of the magazines, radio, TV and websites that compile such lists, this haunting epic signified Prince's true arrival, proving the success he enjoyed from *1999* wasn't just a flash in the pan.

'In some ways, 'Purple Rain' scared me', Prince revealed in an interview with *The Observer* some years later. 'It's my albatross, and it'll be hanging around my neck as long as I'm making music'. But that is the price he had to pay for producing a song of such stature. As important a song as it was for Prince, 'Purple Rain' was just as important for the members of The Revolution. They had gone from an unnamed and largely uncredited backing band to being on the periphery of greatness in the blink of an eye, and in the liner notes of the 2017 reissue, Bobby Z. could barely hide his pride in what 'Purple Rain' had afforded him and his crew:

'Purple Rain' was the song Prince and the Revolution were born to record. Each member of the band added just enough of themselves to make it a whole; all pushed to the edge of what music can do to a soul with one of the most iconic guitar solos in history. Country, gospel, rock and soul all at once, it took on a life of its own that lives in all of us to this very day.

It comes as no surprise to learn that 'Purple Rain' was Prince's most-performed song live, and poignantly, it was the last song he would ever play in concert. On his *Piano & A Microphone* tour, the show at the Fox Theater in Atlanta on 14 April 2016 saw Prince conclude with a stripped-down rendition a million miles from the grandeur of the original, but it remained similarly engrossing. It was impossible to consider at the time, but just seven days later, Prince would be gone.

The Purple Rain Tour

In preparation for taking *Purple Rain* on the road, Prince rented a converted rehearsal space at Flying Cloud Drive. Located at 9025 on the street of the same name in Eden Prairie, the space was only ten miles from the St. Louis Park warehouse.

Prince bought Flying Cloud Drive for $450,000 in spring 1985 before knocking it down with every intention of building a brand-new recording studio in its place. When he realised the area wasn't going to be big enough to meet his demands – not to mention the lack of privacy he would have due to the volume of traffic passing by in such close proximity – Prince gave up on the plot and instead put the wheels in motion for the legendary Paisley Park. Named after the song included on the *Around The World In A Day* album – which was inspired by Prince's love of the Paisley print design the 65,000 square-foot mega-building in Chanhassen would contain two recording studios, a rehearsal studio, a movie soundstage, offices and a new home for Prince himself. Construction of Paisley Park was completed in April 1987 at a reported cost of $10,000,000.

At Flying Cloud Drive, The Revolution were put through the wringer by having to learn lots of new choreography, which they would perform in front of sell-out crowds all over America for the next six months, all while playing their instruments.

After a trial-run concert at the 2500-capacity Bogarts in Detroit on 23 September 1983, the *Purple Rain* tour began at the Joe Louis Arena on 4 November. It was the first of seven shows to be played at the home of the Detroit Red Wings NHL team over nine nights. A total of 98 shows were performed during the six-month trek; however, many more were initially planned before any official announcements were made. Some venues were booked and then cancelled before tickets went on sale, such as the Kemper Arena in Kansas City, where Prince paid $30,000 in damages for the two dates he decided to pull. Other cities, including Pittsburgh, Richmond and Tempe, were also expecting to welcome the tour of the year, but with some venues being deemed too small, Prince's prospective appearances failed to materialise.

The majority of locations where Prince did perform were booked for multiple nights at a time, but the crowds continued to turn up in their droves. Over 1,700,000 tickets were sold overall, and fans were treated to Prince's biggest and boldest stage show yet. Renowned lighting designer LeRoy Bennett began working with Prince on the *Dirty Mind* tour, and in an interview with *Rolling Stone* in 2017, he reminisced about how *Purple Rain* took things to a whole new level:

Purple Rain Prince and the Revolution

The theatrics started to become more and more evident. *Controversy* had a little bit, and the *1999* tour had a bit more theatrics in it. But the *Purple Rain* tour was a major step in technology for us. Once you've seen a laser beam for five minutes, you're done with it. So what we were doing was pushing the lasers and different things through fiber optics. We had dry-ice fog, but we used liquid nitrogen a lot. For 'When Doves Cry', we'd have jets that shot horizontally across the stage and dissipated. Other lights came up from the back like these huge fountains. We wanted the show to be more of an immersive experience. We wanted to portray the emotions of the songs and create interesting environments.

Prince took to the stage via a hydraulic trapdoor, and he debuted two custom-built Telecaster guitars known as 'Ejacucasters', which sprayed a purple-coloured liquid over those in the front rows. There was even a purple bathtub brought onto the stage, made from fibreglass and therefore relatively lightweight. The first time Prince tried out the prop during rehearsals, the bathtub hadn't been properly nailed into the platform, causing it to fall backwards with the star of the show going with it. Fortunately, there were no injuries, just some minor bruising and a great deal of embarrassment. Prince stormed out of the rehearsal without speaking a word to anyone. But if anything, the unfortunate event made sure there would be no repeat disaster when the tour officially began.

Apollonia 6 and Sheila E. were brought along as the support acts. It had been anticipated that The Time would also be on the bill because of their prominent role in the *Purple Rain* movie, but some of their key members had already left the band by this point to pursue new opportunities. Morris Day and Jerome Benton were the most notable absentees.

At the risk of being fined up to $500 by Prince for missing their cue or making a mistake during playing, The Revolution were put through three-hour soundchecks occupying entire afternoons ahead of an 8 pm show time. Saxophonists Eric Leeds and Eddie Mininfield were added to the band for certain parts of the performances, with Leeds later becoming an official member of The Revolution ahead of the *Parade* tour.

As well as Sheila E. and her band joining Prince onstage at times, other guests made cameo appearances as the tour progressed. Prince just happened to follow Bruce Springsteen and Def Leppard from city to city – the Sheffield rockers promoting their 1982 album

Adrenalize, and the Boss delighting his fans with live renditions of songs from his *Born In The U.S.A.* masterpiece. At Prince's Inglewood Forum show on 23 February (which coincided with the 27th annual Grammy Awards held a day later at the Shrine Auditorium in downtown Los Angeles), Springsteen was in attendance and came onstage to play an extended guitar solo during the 'Baby I'm A Star' jam. Madonna was also there that night, and she, too, was invited to join in on the festivities.

Another well-documented show was the stand-alone date at the Carrier Dome in Syracuse on 30 March. By this time, Prince had decided against taking the tour over to Europe. The pressures of fame were beginning to take a toll, and he became more withdrawn and isolated from his bandmates. He was also bored with playing the same songs every night. The Syracuse concert was broadcast live across Europe as part of Westdeutscher Rundfunk's *Rockpalast* series, simply titled *Prince And The Revolution: Live*, and in equal parts a treat and an apology for the fact the tour would not be heading overseas. Released on VHS on 29 July 1985 and on DVD as part of the *Purple Rain* deluxe reissue in 2017, the audio of the show was released on CD and vinyl for the first time (officially) in June 2022 via Legacy Recordings in conjunction with the Prince estate.

The broadcast left some people underwhelmed, though, due to the camera equipment being unable to fully export the exaggerated live show into people's homes in the way it was wished to be projected. In a July 2020 Q&A session with the Prince fan site *housequake.com*, LeRoy Bennett spoke of his disappointment with how the show came across:

I have to admit, the live broadcast for the *Purple Rain* tour was my least favourite of anything we did. We were playing a venue which was much bigger than what the production was designed for, so it felt a bit lost. The TV cameras at the time weren't as sensitive as they are now, so the nuances of colours and light levels never read the way they were live. TV lighting in those days was always bland because of those issues. Prince and I were both disappointed, but there was no way to replicate the feel of the live show in the broadcast, considering the limitations.

The *Purple Rain* shows ran for an average of 100 minutes per night, and attendance averaged around the 20,000 mark. Six dates at the Nassau Coliseum brought in over 100,000 people, while 60,000 attended the one date at the Louisiana Superdome in New Orleans. Over the three shows at the Reunion Arena in Dallas – which saw out 1984 and welcomed in 1985 with a bang – 110,000 jubilant fans celebrated a new year with Prince and the Revolution.

Earning around $30,000,000 in revenue and becoming one of the highest-grossing tours of the year, the *Purple Rain* tour concluded at the Orange Bowl in Miami on 7 April 1985, when for one night only, the outdoor stadium was renamed the Purple Bowl in honour of the headline act.

Setlist for the opening show of the tour at the Joe Louis Arena, Detroit, Michigan (4 November 1984):

'Let's Go Crazy'
'Delirious'
'1999'
'Little Red Corvette'
(Keyboard Interlude)

(Solo Piano Set)
'Free'
'Father's Song'
'God'
'Computer Blue'
'Darling Nikki'
'The Beautiful Ones'
'When Doves Cry'

(Encore)
'I Would Die 4 U'
'Baby I'm A Star'

(Encore 2)
'Purple Rain'

Setlist for the final show of the tour at the Orange Bowl, Miami, Florida (7 April 1985):

'Let's Go Crazy'
'Delirious'
'1999'

'Little Red Corvette'
'Take Me With U'
'Do Me, Baby'
'Irresistible Bitch'
'Possessed'
'How Come U Don't Call Me Anymore'
'Let's Pretend We're Married'
'International Lover'
'God'
'Computer Blue'
'Darling Nikki'
'The Beautiful Ones'
'When Doves Cry'

(Encore)
'I Would Die 4 U'
'Baby I'm A Star'

(Encore 2)
'Purple Rain'

Reception And Commercial Performance

It isn't until the end of a decade that we usually evaluate societal, commercial, economic and environmental progressions, declines and everything in between. The 1920s has frequently been cited as the most important decade in history, especially for Americans, when self-independence came with the advancement of transportation technology, higher personal income, the emergence of credit, and, most culturally significant of all, new freedoms afforded to women.

The 1980s was a huge decade for the US, too. 1981 saw the New Right conservative movement steering further away from the Democratic Party, favouring the economic agenda put forward by Ronald Reagan in his bid to become the 40th President of the United States of America. Reagan's policy pledges – dubbed Reaganomics – and his anti-communist stance on the Cold War enticed enough voters to get him into the White House over Jimmy Carter in 1980. Though America suffered their worst recession since the Great Depression of the 1930s, the stock market crash in 1987 and the rise of the AIDS epidemic – all during his eight-year double term of office – Reagan's legacy was drawn from stimulating economic growth, strengthening the nation's defence system, and helping to bring the Cold War to an end after 45 long years.

Pop culture of the 1980s also reflected the political conservatism of the time. Aside from the Yuppie culture and their proclivity for materialistic wealth, the majority of households spent their evenings glued to TV sets after a long day at work or school, in uncontrollable fits of laughter as they embraced sitcoms such as *Cheers*, *The Golden Girls*, and *The Cosby Show*. The movies *E.T.*, *Ghostbusters*, *Batman*, *Top Gun*, *Back To The Future* and the *Indiana Jones* and *Star Wars* franchises grossed millions at the box office.

But it was music that, for many, offered the biggest development in creative expression. With the launch of MTV, the visual aspect of music became all the more important, putting faces to the songs 24 hours a day, 365 days a year. Artist's appearances, expressions, fashion senses and dance skills became all the more significant with the volume of music videos, concert performances and documentaries which were broadcast into people's homes. The game had changed.

1984 saw remarkable debut albums from Bon Jovi, Frankie Goes to Hollywood, Red Hot Chili Peppers, Run-D.M.C. and The Smiths, all of whom would prove to be pioneers of their chosen genres. Heavy metal continued its devilish rise, helped by MTV, and putting parents on notice as Iron Maiden, Judas Priest, Metallica and Twisted

Sister warped the minds of teenagers who fancied a little rebellion in their lives. And then there was Bruce Springsteen, Madonna, Queen, Wham! and Prince, who had their own singular traits but also possessed an irresistible pop charm in their quest for mainstream dominance. More than anything, though, their music reminded people to simply have fun and express themselves in whichever way they wanted without fear of ridicule.

Ahead of and upon its release, *Purple Rain* was met with critical acclaim. It was praised for its innovative instrumentation and the successful amalgamations of electronics with traditional guitars, bass and drums through full-band participation. The album was also lauded for its experimental and, at times, complex compositions. In a review by *Rolling Stone*, Prince was compared to Jimi Hendrix in terms of how he was able to merge black and white musical styles. In relation to the movie, the publication later called *Purple Rain* 'an epic celebration of everything rock & roll, which means sex and religion and eyeliner and motorcycles and guitars and Lake Minnetonka'. Ben Greenmane discussed how the album propelled Prince to 'Supernova' status and how the ruffled shirts and purple jackets worn in the film created his iconic look. Even esteemed musicians such as Jon Bon Jovi and Lionel Richie praised *Purple Rain* for its outstanding ingenuity. There were a handful of negative reviews by those who continued to misinterpret Prince's creative spirit, but it is fair to say the album, on the whole, was met with overwhelming positivity.

After debuting at 11 on the *Billboard* 200 on 14 July, *Purple Rain* went to number one on 4 August, replacing Springsteen's *Born In The U.S.A.,* and remaining on top for the next 24 weeks. Incredibly, only five albums topped the chart in the whole of 1984 – Michael Jackson's *Thriller* (for 15 straight weeks), the *Footloose* movie soundtrack (ten weeks), Huey Lewis and the News' *Sports* (one week), *Born In The U.S.A.* (four weeks), and then *Purple Rain* for the remainder of 1984. With the accompanying movie also at number one by the time 'When Doves Cry' ascended to the top of the Hot 100, Prince became only the third artist ever to have the number-one song, album and movie at the same time in America, joining Elvis Presley and The Beatles on a short but illustrious roll of honour.

Born In The U.S.A. ousted *Purple Rain* to return to number one on 19 January 1985. But in all, Prince's fifth opus spent 32 weeks in the top ten and 120 weeks on the chart in total. Within seven months of its release, the album had already been certified nine times platinum, and in February 1989, it was officially given diamond status for surpassing 10,000,000 in sales. Today, the figure stands at over 13,000,000. *Purple Rain* also went to number one on the top R&B/Hip-Hop Albums in America and in the national charts of Australia, Canada, the Netherlands and Zimbabwe. In the UK, the album peaked at seven and remained on the chart for 86 consecutive weeks.

One of the best-selling soundtracks of all time, and with worldwide sales of over 25,000,000 at present, *Purple Rain* was also recognised at the Grammys and was nominated for three awards in 1985. Missing out on the Album of the Year award, the record did scoop the Best Score Soundtrack for Visual Media award, while the Best Rock Vocal Performance by a Duo or Group with Vocal prize went directly to Prince and the Revolution. Incidentally, Prince earned a further Grammy that night when 'I Feel For You' (which featured on his self-titled 1979 album) won Best R&B Song. Covered by Chaka Khan in 1984, the track reached three on the Hot 100 and was actually thwarted from moving any higher due to the battle taking place between 'Purple Rain' and Wham!'s 'Wake Me Up Before You Go-Go'. Still, 'I Feel For You' helped revive Khan's career, and she also scooped a Grammy in 1985 for Best R&B Vocal Performance by a Female. *Purple Rain* also secured an Oscar in the same year – for Best Original Song Score, confirming the album had most definitely lived up to its billing.

Variations, Reissues And B-Sides

Since its original release, *Purple Rain* has had plenty of standard reissues over the years. From cassette and 8-track tapes to CDs and vinyl, the album has also been pressed as a picture disc and, unsurprisingly, a purple-coloured LP, and the releases have often come with posters and stickers – but very little else.

At the end of 1984, a promotional double-LP compilation titled *Strange Tales From The Rain* was issued in Japan with no intention of being sold to the wider public. The first disc contained the songs used in the movie and in the sequence they appeared, thus including The Time's 'Jungle Love' and 'The Bird', and Apollonia 6's 'Sex Shooter' – all three of which were written by Prince. Presumably, because of the limited space on vinyl and to be able to fit all the songs on four sides, 'Purple Rain' appeared in its 4:02 radio edit form. The second LP was comprised of Prince's hits up to *Purple Rain,* and in the order they had been released, beginning with 'Soft And Wet' from the *For You* album, culminating in 'Delirious' from *1999.* The final song on the disc was Sheila E.'s 'The Glamorous Life' – written by Prince and released in 1984 – but still, it seemed a rather strange inclusion. A handful of copies of *Strange Tales From The Rain* can still be found online, but they do not come cheap. A couple of other notable releases include a box set from 1990, which was exclusive to Germany and contained the album on CD, the movie on VHS tape, and a poster. In 1997, *Purple Rain* was pressed on 180g heavyweight vinyl for the first time, with European-only distribution.

The one thing all of these reissues had in common was that none of them presented any new songs, and with Prince the tireless workaholic everyone knew him to be, it was widely acknowledged that there was a lot of unreleased material being withheld from his adoring fan base. Some of the songs may have been available online or in bootleg form, but people wanted to physically own them and in the best sound quality possible.

Purple Rain-era B-sides found their way onto the 'When Doves Cry', 'Let's Go Crazy', 'Purple Rain' and 'I Would Die 4 U' singles, and after Prince revealed to *Rolling Stone* in 1985 that he had a lot more material hidden away in his now famous vault, fans were excited to find out what else was recorded during those sessions. It may have taken some time, but all prayers were finally answered with the reissue of all reissues in 2017. The world was still coming to terms with Prince's death at this time, and though the release was planned to coincide with the album's 30th anniversary in 2014, its long-awaited arrival three years later felt like Prince's ultimate parting gift.

The deluxe edition came as a two-CD package, but it was the four-disc expanded edition that the majority of consumers were most excited about. There were no surprises on the first disc: *Purple Rain* in its traditional running order. The songs were remastered by Bernie Grundman at Paisley Park Studios in 2015, with Prince overseeing the whole process. Disc two *From the Vault & Previously Unreleased* offered 11 tracks recorded between April and September 1984. Part of the *Purple Rain* sessions before and after the album's completion and release, it has been presumed that almost none of the songs were ever intended to be included on the album at any point. The third disc *Single Edits & B-sides* was exactly what the title suggested; the singles especially found here in the edited forms from their 7" vinyl releases. There were also a few B-sides on the disc, and they will be discussed in due course. The fourth and final disc presented the full Syracuse concert from 30 March 1985, originally broadcast live in Europe. Appearing here on DVD for the first time, the show was given new life due to the audio and video being restored from the original production master tape.

From The Vault & Previously Unreleased
'The Dance Electric' (Prince)
A rousing and funky number possessing a pulsing drum rhythm, raunchy guitar licks and subtle synth, 'The Dance Electric' is classic Prince and appropriate for the time when it was written. Recorded by Prince alone at the Flying Cloud Drive warehouse on 17 August, it is this version which found its way onto the 2017 reissue, and not the one with vocal overdubs by Wendy, Lisa and Jill Jones.

With 'The Dance Electric', Prince implores us all to love our enemies; the song's overall theme of putting aside personal differences and showing unity comes across as strong in its delivery. It isn't the most potent message the purple one ever put across, but at a time when the world was struggling, this spirited track at least helped people dance their troubles away for a while. It wouldn't be Prince's version that brought people together, though. In 1985, he gave the song to his old buddy André Cymone, whom he had known since the seventh grade. The pair grew up together in Minneapolis, sharing dreams of becoming famous musicians and, at one point, even becoming roommates for a short time when Prince moved into Cymone's family home following a fallout with his father. As a talented bass player, Cymone had formed Grand Central with Prince, and later, he was recruited to play in Prince's first touring band in the summer of 1978. That lineup was completed by Dez Dickerson, Bobby Z., Matt Fink and Gayle Chapman. Cymone left the band in 1981, having signed a record deal with Columbia as a solo artist, and it was with his third album *A.C.* in 1985 that his big break came. Cymone's mother had reportedly asked Prince if he would give her son one of his songs, as young André was far too proud to ask for himself. Prince duly obliged, passing over 'The Dance Electric'. With the instrumentation already in place, Cymone recorded his vocals at Ocean Way in Hollywood on 15 May 1985 with Prince in attendance. Released a month before *A.C.*, 'The Dance Electric' reached ten on *Billboard*'s R&B chart. But the relationship between Cymone and Prince soon turned sour when Prince repeatedly spoke of how the song was his own work. *A.C.* would be Cymone's last album for almost 30 years, his disillusionment from the Prince fallout finding him retreating from the spotlight and taking on a new career as a record producer. In 2012, the friends reunited on stage during a concert Prince was performing in Los Angeles and playing 'The Dance Electric' together; it felt just like old times.

On the seventh episode of his monthly download service he called the NPG Ahdio Show in 2001, Prince released a May 1986 live recording of this sonic disco jam. As good as the song is, its 11:29 running time is a tad long, especially with its repetitive instrumental cycle. It may have had Prince's stamp all over it, but Cymone's six-minute version offers a more fulfilling listening experience, and its wider release meant people could come together on dance floors and vibe as if their lives depended on it.

'Love And Sex' (Prince)
Recorded on 27 February 1984 at Sunset Sound, 'Love And Sex' finds its writer questioning whether he and his lover will be able to have sex in the afterlife.

Feeling very much like a live recording and capturing the song's urgency, 'Love And Sex' is unerringly synth-heavy. For the song, Prince wanted to use a Yamaha DX7, so he sent Peggy McCreary out to buy one. Evidently happy with what the synthesizer could do, the song sounds like Prince experimented with every function made available to him, and he used the DX7 on many later songs in his career.

In January 1986, Prince recorded a new song of the same name, this time a mid-tempo guitar-driven number, which would later be released on the 2020 super deluxe edition of *Sign O' The Times*. A faster and groovier version of the song was recorded in 1986 for Sheila E. with every intention of including it on her self-titled third album. However, the song was withdrawn at some point.

The *Purple Rain*-era 'Love And Sex' was certainly in keeping with what Prince was coming up with in 1984: vibrant and fun pop. But its omission from the original album feels like the correct choice. Its presence on the 2017 reissue is far more welcome, and the song made for one of the best additions of all the vault tracks.

'Electric Intercourse' (Prince)

Until its release in 2017, it was believed a studio version of 'Electric Intercourse' did not exist. A bootlegged live/rehearsal recording from July 1983 had been doing the rounds for years, as had a 3 August First Avenue performance which Prince later added some overdubs to. Hidden deep inside his Paisley Park vault was this little gem, though, sparser in sound, but a studio recording nonetheless, and all Prince's own work.

A feisty ballad revolving around erotic electricity, Prince's lyrics contain plenty of double entendre ('sexual current', 'technicolor climax'), which, had 'Electric Intercourse' been given greater exposure back in 1984, could also have found its way onto the PMRC's naughty list alongside 'Darling Nikki'. In a 2004 interview with *The Washington Post*, Prince discussed the controversy some of his lyrics caused in the early part of his career:

> Times were different back then. I wouldn't stand out today if I was brand new and came like that. But see, back then, nobody else was doing that, and I knew that would get me over. I didn't dress like anybody, I didn't look like anybody, I didn't sound like anybody.

Musically guided by romantic piano riffs and swooning synths, with Prince's seductive double-tracked vocal slathered on top, 'Electric Intercourse' is the one song that was considered for inclusion on *Purple Rain* before ultimately being bumped in favour of 'The Beautiful Ones'. Still, this studio take came as a nice surprise when it was released as a digital single on 28 April 2017, six weeks before the reissue's arrival. The track was also sent to those who pre-ordered the reissue as an 'instant gratitude'.

'Our Destiny/Roadhouse Garden' (Prince)

Though worked on separately in the studio, 'Our Destiny' and 'Roadhouse Garden' appear as one here, segued together as they were when performed in the live environment.

Disparate in sound and style but both following the same 4/4 rhythm, the sweetly innocent 'Our Destiny' begins with a very similar string section to that which drew 'Purple Rain' to its close. The string arrangement was created by Wendy and Lisa at Sunset Sound in September 1984, during which time they were also working on 'Pop Life' for *Around The World In A Day*. Boasting a large cast for the orchestral parts – including Suzie Katayama and David Coleman on cello duties once again – the additional violinists, saxophonists and those brought in for the horns, trumpets and upright bass made for a rather complex recording process considering the song's intended B-side status.

The most intriguing aspect of 'Our Destiny' comes with hearing Lisa taking on lead vocals. In fact, the song is the earliest recorded track to feature such. Prince had laid down his lead on an earlier version, itself growing from an early piano demo. But for whatever reason, he felt a female voice made for better storytelling on this occasion. He even had Jill Jones record lead vocals too – on a song about falling in love but erring on the side of caution so as not to fall too deeply in love so soon – before Prince decided to go with Lisa's impressive contribution.

'Our Destiny' was initially recorded live at a First Avenue concert on 7 June 1984, which Prince played on his 26th birthday. Effortlessly segueing into 'Roadhouse Garden' – for which basic tracking also took place at that same First Avenue show – the synth and keyboard melodies float around a repeated rhythm and in an increased tempo compared to that of its predecessor; the track changing course as Prince returns to the mic and sings of a dreamy landscape where personal and artistic expression can thrive.

A number of albums have been put together by Prince which have never seen the light of day, and *Roadhouse Garden* is one of them. Supposedly comprised of unfinished songs he and The Revolution worked on before their split in 1986, the album was plotted in 1998 or 1999 and would likely have been centred around this choice cut. Part of the strings from 'Our Destiny' were later incorporated into 'The Ladder', found on *Around The World In A Day*, while the frequent 'It's alright, it's alright' refrain on 'Roadhouse Garden' can also be heard on the *Sign O' The Times* track 'It'. This fascinating doubleheader was the second single released to promote the reissue.

'Possessed' (1984 Version) (Prince)

After attending a James Brown concert, Prince went home and wrote the sexy and swaggering 'Possessed', and the godfather of funk and soul's inspiration is evident throughout the whole song.

A studio version was tracked at Kiowa Trail sometime in 1982 before an extended live jam made its debut on the *1999* tour. From there, the track was completely rewritten with The Revolution at The Warehouse in August 1983, and in this instance, 'Possessed' expressed itself through a robo-funk groove, abrasive guitars and punchy synths. As Prince sings of being lovesick to the point of going crazy, the 1983 version included some lyrics which seemed a tad overzealous in getting the point across: 'You know what that means/Pussy getting wet'. In fact, come March of the following year, when Prince was back at Sunset Sound, 'Possessed' was given yet another overhaul.

While the earlier takes were methodically paced and fulfilling, the one added to the reissue is more hyped, upbeat, experimental and obtuse. The guitars and bass had been completely removed by this time, making way for a synth and keyboard lead over a funky programmed beat. The instrumentation actually mimics the craziness of the song's theme, even if the lyrics were toned down a little. But the idea of love leading someone to insanity remains firmly at the forefront of proceedings. The interlude 'Have you ever had the feeling like someone was tearing you up into little bitty pieces and contemplating selling you for a jigsaw puzzle?' is unexpected, to say the least, but its expressive delivery is absolutely masterful and makes for one of the song's standout moments.

'Possessed' hits eight minutes but rarely changes flow or pace, while Prince's vocal gets ever the more theatrical. It's interesting to hear the song's progression over the three recordings, which came in the space of just two short years. But it is the 1983 version that most fans continue to hold in the highest regard. It is one of the most beloved songs from the vault, and although 'Possessed' wasn't played on the early dates, it did become a staple in setlists on the *Purple Rain* tour.

A short instrumental piece of the song can be heard in the movie during the First Avenue scene where The Revolution are about to perform 'The Beautiful Ones' and The Kid watches on as Morris Day attempts to seduce Apollonia.

'Wonderful Ass' (Prince)

Another frequently bootlegged fan favourite vault number, 'Wonderful Ass' is presumed to be Prince's love letter to Vanity's posterior. The song could even have been considered for *Purple Rain* had Vanity not split from Prince and walked away from the whole project in its early stages.

Recorded in either late 1982 or early 1983 with Jill Jones at Kiowa Trail, the mid-tempo pop-funk romp was given further treatment in or around September '84 when Wendy and Lisa added vocal overdubs. On the reissue version, their backing vocals are actually higher in the mix, and their tag team overshadows Prince's refrain, slightly taking away from the cheeky (pardon the pun) but personal ode the purple one had invented.

Though uncredited, Jill Jones deserves a mention for assisting Prince with the rhyming section midway through, coming up with some of the entries in this singular word barrage:

Educate, tolerate, negotiate, communicate
Litigate, graduate, appreciate, separate
Interrogate, violate, fluctuate, perpetrate
Masturbate, stimulate, stimulate, stimulate

Sporting a complex drum-machine pattern, jangling guitar fills and laser-like waves of synth, 'Wonderful Ass' is another song later tipped to appear on the shunned *Roadhouse Garden* album. It was also previously considered for use on Vanity 6, Apollonia 6 and The Time records. In 2016, Victor DeLorenzo from Wisconsin rockers Violent Femmes revealed that Prince offered 'Wonderful Ass' to the band in 1991. Both artists had been in the same studio with Susan Rogers at the time, but the Femmes declined the song while they continued to prepare their fifth album, *Why Do Birds Sing?*

In a 2017 interview with the *Star Tribune*, Lisa Coleman spoke of the song actually being about Wendy and Susannah Melvoin. Prince was dating Susannah, and Lisa was dating Wendy during the song's creation. But with Prince's complicated history with Vanity and a host of other women, 'Wonderful Ass' could really have been written about any or every single one of them.

'Velvet Kitty Cat' (Prince)

'She's a man's best friend/Furry and cuddly and fat' sings Prince with tongue in cheek on a sub-three-minute song about vaginas – or more specifically, Susan Moonsie's, it is believed.

An update of the never-released 'Mink Kitty Cat' from 1981, 'Velvet Kitty Cat' was tracked in April 1983 at Sunset Sound while

Prince was producing The Time's *Ice Cream Castle* album. Never considered for inclusion in *Purple Rain*, the song was thrown out to The Time, Vanity 6 and, latterly, Apollonia 6, but there were no takers.

Very much a throwaway track and one of the weakest in Prince's entire catalogue, 'Velvet Kitty Cat' is sparse and uninspired. With flat guitars, plodding synths and a simple drum rhythm created by a Roland TR-606 Drumatix for the one and only time in Prince's career, the demo feel to this song falls short in comparison to the rockabilly version recorded in 1985, which at one point was set to feature on the *Parade* album. Even diehard fans pretend this one doesn't exist.

'Katrina's Paper Dolls' (Prince)

Another Vanity project, 'Katrina's Paper Dolls', is Prince's solo effort in which he hints at feeling guilt over his non-monogamous relationship with Denise Matthews. A power couple in many ways, the pair's tumultuous time together was marred by Prince's desire to pursue other women at the same time, and the lyrics of this pure pop number appear to be written from the perspective of a lonely Vanity. 'Katrina makes paper dolls/One doll for every day her old man's been gone', sings Prince in his classic storytelling pose, perhaps for the first time contemplating how his actions affected a woman he deeply loved but couldn't necessarily show just how much.

On an off day during the *1999* tour in March 1983, Prince checked himself into Studio B at the Universal Recording Corporation in Chicago. For a long time, a demo of 'Katrina's Paper Dolls' was the only recording readily available until this live studio take was added to the 2017 reissue. A strong song in its own right but not containing anything particularly explosive musically, the fruitful fusion of keys and a prosperous beat at least make for a pretty-sounding studio exercise.

'We Can Fuck' (Prince)

This is the first incarnation of the song, which would become 'We Can Funk' – far more widely known for its George Clinton guest feature and being one of the standout songs on the 1990 *Graffiti Bridge* soundtrack album.

Recorded on New Year's Eve 1983 at Sunset Sound, and with early working titles of 'The Dawn' and 'Moral Majority', 'We Can Fuck' became a brilliantly raunchy and groovy ten-minute epic which expands on the complex experimentation of 'Computer Blue'. Boasting some Middle-Eastern vibrancy from Prince's first foray into using finger cymbals and the oud instrument, further psychedelic nuances revealed a new direction he was planning to explore post-*Purple Rain*.

'We Can Fuck' speaks of instant sexual attraction via moody and throbbing bass, a potent drum beat, haywire synth and keys and piano, which change the song's shape at the halfway point. Prince's vocals are typically enticing, from his sultry and smooth refrains to some instantly recognisable shrieks and wholehearted wails as the song builds to its climax.

In 1986, the song was rerecorded and stripped of its naughtiness for yet another aborted Prince and the Revolution album known to be titled *Dream Factory*. Three years later, 'We Can Funk' was further updated at Paisley Park in preparation for *Graffiti Bridge*: the movie sequel to *Purple Rain*. *Graffiti Bridge* was never going to be as popular or successful as its groundbreaking predecessor, but 'We Can Funk' was at least one of the best songs to come out of the whole project.

'Father's Song' (Prince, John L. Nelson)
The first official release of 'Father's Song' came as a digital single on 16 June 2017, as the most expansive reissue of *Purple Rain* continued to be promoted. A beautiful solo piano piece which Prince built on from his father's incisive melody, it is utilised in the movie during a scene in which 'The Kid' finds his father – a faded former musician – playing the melody on his own piano hidden down in the basement.

Prince recorded the full track at Kiowa Trail on 24 October 1983, and it was planned to be included on *Purple Rain* during early configurations. His contribution to 'Father's Song' is haunting and pained, echoing those fraught father/son relationships in both reality and on the big screen. The dizzying keys, which were later layered over the piano, mirror the main melody, but they don't really need to be there because the piano does enough on its own to paint a pensive backstory.

While the main melody was later added to 'Computer Blue', 'Father's Song' offers an insight into how the track came to be in its full form, in equal parts emitting melancholy, symbolism and hope of repairing fractured relationships.

Single Edits & B-Sides
'17 Days (The Rain Will Come Down, Then U Will Have 2 Choose. If U Believe Look 2 The Dawn And U Shall Never Lose)' (Prince and the Revolution)

Born out of a jam session where Prince began singing a melody over an infectious Lisa Coleman organ riff, '17 Days' would go on to become a huge fan favourite despite only ever being known as a B-side. First recorded at The Warehouse in August 1983 – a time when Vanity had moved on and Patricia Kotero was yet to audition and evolve into Apollonia – Brenda Bennett stepped in to provide some harmony vocals for a song earmarked for the second Vanity 6 album. As he did on many occasions, though, Prince kept '17 Days' for himself, re-recording the track in January 1984 at Sunset Sound. Wendy and Lisa added backing vocals, while some of Bennett's earlier contributions were left in for further posture. Dr. Fink also provided some input on this song, ultimately credited to the whole of The Revolution.

The story of a man coming to terms with his lover leaving him ('All I've got is two cigarettes and this broken heart of mine'), it wasn't the first time Prince had written of heartbreaking loss, and it wouldn't be the last. In a 2018 interview with *The Guardian*, Lisa Coleman spoke of her former leader's yin-and-yang personalities:

He sang the part of the lonely person a lot, like 'When You Were Mine' or 'The Beautiful Ones'. Even though he's got the prowess of a love god, an incredible kind of fantasy person, at the same time, he's like a deer in headlights, a very vulnerable person. Those big brown eyes would kill you.

'17 Days' quickly drew the affection of Prince's followers when it arrived as the B-side of 'When Doves Cry', and the song earned significant airplay on R&B radio and in dance clubs across the US, so much so that it even charted on *Billboard*'s Hot Dance Club Play for a short time. Very few B-sides achieved such acclaim. Upon 'When Doves Cry' climbing its way to the top of the Hot 100, history was made, as '17 Days' – with its full title of 'The Rain Will Come Down, Then U Will Have 2 Choose. If U Believe Look 2 The Dawn And U Shall Never Lose' – became the longest-titled song to appear on the B-side of a number-one record in America. That feat still stands today.

On the posthumously released *Piano & A Microphone* album from 2018, a 1983 piano-rehearsal version of '17 Days' offers a far more intimate and alternative listening experience. It was even released as a 7" single, coming cover-mounted with the October 2018 issue of the German *Rolling Stone* publication. Regularly played live in its various forms up until Prince's death, whoever thought the simple chorus line 'Let the rain come down down' could be so painfully effective?

'Erotic City' (Prince and the Revolution)

A sleazy funk pop gem, 'Erotic City' first announced itself on the 'Let's Go Crazy' single. Built around a synth effect to make the drum track sound reversed and a simple keyboard riff, Prince's experimentation with vocal effects found him speeding up and slowing down his deliveries at various times, making him sound like two different singers. At the same time, his guitar notes and whammy rhythms add some steamy musical verve.

Its inspiration coming from Prince witnessing Parliament-Funkadelic in concert at the Beverly Theater in 1983, 'Erotic City' was the first song to feature collaborative input from Sheila E., arriving just six weeks after the release of her Prince-produced debut album *The Glamorous Life*. Credited to The Revolution, despite having only Prince and Sheila contribute, the duo rose to the fore on this naughty but nice number.

Tracked at Sunset Sound on 25 March 1984, and containing the lines 'We can fuck until the dawn', 'Fuck so pretty you and me' and 'I just want your creamy thighs', it's interesting to think radio stations actually played 'Erotic City' well into the 1990s, and they actually got away with doing so. Sheila E. went on record to say the repeated 'We can fuck until the dawn' line was actually 'We can *funk*'. And while the song title couldn't have exercised a more glaring warning, nor could the brazenly obvious sexual inference enlisted throughout. The radio stations took Sheila's revelation as gospel, and so they continued to play it. From 2004, however, with threats of fines looming over anyone who played songs with obscenities on national radio, those who continued to rotate 'Erotic City' have done so via an edit in which the second section of lyrics was replaced by a repeated first stanza. If further proof was required of the song's original content and intent, Prince's handwritten lyric for 'Erotic City' was sold for just under $45,000 by Juliens Auctions in 2014, and lo-and-behold, there wasn't a 'funk' anywhere in sight.

A second version with the extended 'Make Love Not War Erotic City Come Alive' title can be found on the Special Dance Mix 12" of

'Let's Go Crazy' and on the reissue's *Single Edits & B-sides* disc. With a running time of 7:24, the musical ingredients remain the same but are further drawn out. There are some small lyric additions, but in all honesty, the 3:55 track packs all the substance that is required.

In 1985, 'Erotic City' was released as a UK-only 12" promo single. A year later, it appeared as the B-side of the 'Girls & Boys' single, the fourth of which was issued to promote the soundtrack album *Parade*, which was the counterpart to *Under The Cherry Moon*: a romantic musical comedy in which Prince acts and makes his directorial debut. Distributed by Warner Bros. and also starring Francesca Annis, Steven Berkoff, and Kristin Scott Thomas in her first feature film, the movie was nowhere near as successful as *Purple Rain*, and its reviews and box-office performance were underwhelming, to say the least. *Parade,* on the other hand, sold over 1,000,000 copies in America alone, thanks in part to the song 'Kiss', which also shifted 1,000,000 units and spent two weeks atop the Hot 100.

The 12" release of 'Girls & Boys' also featured the extended version of 'Erotic City' in all its sordid glory, and in 1989, a dance mix was released in Germany on a 3" mini CD. In 1996, the song was included on the soundtrack of the Spike Lee-directed *Girl 6* movie, its plot surrounding a wannabe female actress who turns to working as a phone sex operator. The tracklist was made up completely of songs by Prince and associated acts such as The Family and New Power Generation.

'God' (Prince)

Like 'Erotic City', 'God' was presented on the *Purple Rain* reissue in two iterations, but they couldn't be more different from one another. The first to be released was the vocal version, as the B-side of the 'Purple Rain' single, where Prince unleashed his spiritual side with an opening passage, an interpretation of the book of Genesis. 'In the beginning, there was God/He made the earth and the heavens/He gave us light to rule the day/And another light to rule the night' sings Prince, sounding like a pastor delivering a Sunday sermon. Over a suave piano piece and orchestral synth, the purple one puts on a vocal masterclass, singing, screaming and everything in between, on a smooth and drumless slow burner.

Tracked six months earlier in February 1984 at Sunset Sound, the eight-minute 'God (Love Theme From *Purple Rain*)' is the polar opposite of the vocal recording. An instrumental where Prince goes guitar hero once again, his bluesy riffs and flashy solos sound effortless, as at every turn, a new lick exudes optimum sensuality. Sheila E.'s drumming is also a highlight, emphasising her skill behind a kit at a time when her solo singing career was beginning to take off. With some subtle piano and dreamy synths, the instrumental has far less of a religious feel compared to the 'God made you/God made me/He made us all/Equally' recital of the Flying Cloud Drive vocal track. There is a certain romanticism to it, in fact, which is hardly surprising when you consider the instrumental was used in the *Purple Rain* movie for The Kid and Apollonia's steamy basement-bedroom sex scene.

'Another Lonely Christmas' (Prince and the Revolution)
The final B-side released as part of the 2017 reissue is an absolute tearjerker, a story of fiction according to Prince, but an emotional and heartbreaking tale, nonetheless.

'Last night I spent another lonely Christmas/Darling, darling, you should've been there', sings Prince – the narrator whose perfect world was torn apart when, seven years prior, his lover passed away on 25 December. 'Another Lonely Christmas' is an absorbing rock ballad, led by a pretty piano lead and, at times, raging guitar, and the song is extremely rich in its production. The grief and reflection poured into the lyrics are some of Prince's finest, in some ways comparable to those of 'Nothing Compares 2 U', which he wrote in less than an hour in 1985. That song was made famous around the world when it was covered by Sinéad O'Connor in 1990, the Irish singer's stunning rendition topping singles charts all around the world (including the UK and US) and achieving sales of over 3,500,000.

The B-side of 'I Would Die 4 U', 'Another Lonely Christmas' was recorded on 18 February 1984. Again, it was credited to The Revolution despite it being a solo Prince effort. The original and extended mix was included on the 12" 'I Would Die 4 U' single, featuring a nice guitar solo and a punchy drum piece. The 4:54 edit did have one other release: a strange Japan-only promo with the alternate title 'Syndicate' distributed purely to radio stations. 'Another Lonely Christmas' is the only song on it, but it is accompanied by some short messages intended to precede the playing of specific songs on the radio. Sheila E. introduces her song 'The Belle Of St. Mark', Apollonia welcomes 'Sex Shooter' and 'Blue Limousine', and Prince sets the scene for the resplendent 'Purple Rain'.

The only time 'Another Lonely Christmas' was played live was during Prince's 26 December 1984 concert in Saint Paul, Minnesota.

'We'd like to give you a Christmas present right now', Prince said to the crowd beforehand, and you can only imagine the reaction the performance received (unless someone reading this was in attendance that night).

A mournful ballad depicting irreplaceable loss and made all the more sublime by Prince's entrancing vocal, 'Another Lonely Christmas' is another song of fantastic quality. As with some of his other B-sides, it is staggering how such songs were deemed unsuitable for wider releases. With so much more material remaining hidden away in his legendary vault, one can only imagine what other masterpieces Prince has kept from the world for so long – based on those that have gone on to see the light of day.

The Legacy Of Purple Rain

Purple Rain is widely regarded as one of the greatest albums of all time, and yet it may not even be Prince's *pièce de résistance*. *1999* put the artist on the map, led by the prophetic party anthem title track and 'Little Red Corvette', which brought a whole new audience upon MTV's belated show of inclusivity. The album itself was packed full of hypnotic grooves and vibrant beats, created by Prince's impressive exploitation of the latest drum machines on the market. And then there is *Sign O' The Times,* released in 1987 on the back of the somewhat surprisingly triumphant *Parade. Sign O' The Times* fulfilled Prince's lofty ambitions, even if his planned triple album was ultimately scaled down to a double – much to the artist's initial disdain. However, it still contained plenty of sexy soul, imposing funk, rousing rockers and other songs which, in musical terms, defied logic and categorisation. *Sign O' The Times* was a diverse but consistently brilliant affair, finding Prince exploring an array of socio-political themes where, at times, his words stood taller than the music. The title track is a perfect example of less being more.

This book, however, is dedicated to *Purple Rain,* now 40 years old and with a legacy as strong as any of his other work that came before or after. Culturally significant and culturally important, *Purple Rain* announced itself at a time of great economic and societal change. In a retrospective review of the album for *Billboard* in 2014, Kenneth Partridge began his feature with this defining statement: 'In 1984, there was only one man in America more popular than Ronald Reagan. His name was Prince, and he was funky'. Partridge wasn't wrong, and while half the world had been thinking the same thing since the 1980s, the journalist had finally written it in print.

From the oppressive and eyebrow-raising instrumentation (or lack of) of 'When Doves Cry', to the controversial lyrics and landmark response surrounding 'Darling Nikki', and the host of funk-fuelled dance-floor hymns that came in between before the ballad of all ballads brought *Purple Rain* to a close, here was a body of work by an artist who was way ahead of the curve in terms of innovation.

Rolling Stone ranked *Purple Rain* at number two in their 100 Best Albums of the 1980s (behind The Clash's *London Calling*) and in the same position on their 25 Greatest Soundtracks list. The Beatles' *Help!* came first on that occasion. In 2008, *Entertainment Weekly* placed *Purple Rain* at the top of their 100 Best Albums of the Previous 25 Years, while in 2016, *Billboard* took on the task of ranking all 92 diamond-selling albums from worst to best based on critics' choices. Featuring some of music's most groundbreaking works – Michael Jackson's *Thriller*, Nirvana's *Nevermind*, Pink Floyd's *The Wall* and Madonna's *Like A Virgin* included – it was *Purple Rain* that ranked as the absolute best of them all.

In 2011, *Purple Rain* was inducted into the Grammy Hall of Fame, seven years after Prince himself had been entered into the Rock and Roll Hall of Fame. Incidentally, in 2004, the organisation created the 500 Songs That Shaped Rock and Roll list, where 'When Doves Cry' and 'Little Red Corvette' were both recognised. A further 160 songs were added in 2018, including two more of Prince's: 'Purple Rain' and 'Sign O' The Times'.

A year after *Purple Rain* went into the Grammy Hall of Fame for its 'lasting qualitative or historical significance', the nine-track opus was added to the Library of Congress's National Recording Registry's list of sound recordings considered culturally, historically or aesthetically important. For the same reasons, the associated movie was selected for preservation in the United States National Film Registry in 2019.

In an interview with *Ebony* back in 1986, Prince stated:

I think *Purple Rain* is the most avant-garde purple thing I've ever done. I'm not saying that I'm great or anything like that; I'm just saying that I'm an alternative. I'm something else.

Prince was indeed an alternative, and there was no one else like him. Frequently compared to Michael Jackson throughout the 1980s, Prince was also competing with Madonna, Bruce Springsteen and a wealth of pop talent throughout his most successful decade. His biggest moment came in the form of *Purple Rain*, and the success the entire project generated is there for all to see. The movie raked in over $70,000,000 at the box office. It wasn't the best feature film out there, but its vision and audacious delivery, set in motion by a musician who revealed himself to be so much more, reacted with audiences of whom some had likely never appreciated Prince's resourcefulness beforehand. And then the album – which again many believe isn't even Prince's best work, but its timing was perfect in conquering a target audience while also reeling in new fans from the rock world, his virtuosic guitar-playing coming as a shock to many. It was during the *Purple Rain* tour when the shift in his core audience evidently took place, and a large proportion would stay along for the ride in the years that followed.

Over the last four decades, countless artists have covered the songs from *Purple Rain*. The Foo Fighters, fronted by former Nirvana icon Dave Grohl, have regularly performed 'Darling Nikki' during their shows, as well as recording a studio version, which can be found on their 'Have It All' single from 2003. The track is also part of the band's 2011 covers album *Medium Rare*. Prince clearly approved, so much so that during his incredible Superbowl XLI half-time show in 2007, he responded with a blazing cover of the Foo's massive hit song 'Best Of You'.

LeAnn Rimes, Etta James, Eric Clapton and heavy-metallers Virgin Steele are just a few to have taken on the almighty task of covering 'Purple Rain'. Some put an interesting spin on the song, while others followed the same blueprint in an ode to a classic. The Swedish punks Refused, alt-rockers Incubus and British boy band 911 have all taken on 'Let's Go Crazy', as has Janelle Mónae, who earlier in her career was mentored by the purple one. The Kansas singer-songwriter performed a storming interpretation of the *Purple Rain* opener at the 2010 BET Awards, where Prince received a lifetime achievement honour.

'When Doves Cry' is perhaps the most covered song of the bunch by a host of artists from all genres. From Razorlight to Damien Rice and Patti Smith to Nonpoint, most versions have done themselves justice. But when R&B singer Ginuwine took on the mega-hit in 1996, he earned the wrath of the song's creator. 'He didn't even get the groove right', said Prince rather scathingly.

There has also been a small handful of tribute albums recorded over the years. In 2004, a symphonic tribute by the Eaton Canyon Royal Ensemble presented exactly what its title suggested. It appears these albums came out at the time of a significant anniversary – much like this book, although its arrival just as *Purple Rain* turns 40 is nothing more than a happy accident. The digital-only *Purplish Rain* – put together by *Spin* magazine in July 2009 to tie in with the 25th anniversary of Prince's masterpiece – features the likes of Mariachi El Bronx, Riverboat Gamblers, Chairlift and the band of Montreal covering some of the album's nine tracks.

The most interesting tribute album came in 2014, when Brian Leiser and Frank Benbini, from the New York rap-rock trio Fun Lovin' Criminals, combined their love of reggae and dub with a healthy dose of Prince admiration to create *Purple Reggae*. Under the moniker Radio Riddler, and releasing the album via MITA Records, the set of extremely fun and chilled covers includes guest musicians such as Suggs from Madness, Ali Campbell from UB40, and even Sinéad O'Connor. 'Computer Blue' and 'When Doves Cry' are standouts, while the slant from which 'Purple Rain' is presented is very different from how most of us perceive the song. *Purple Reggae* is definitely worth a listen, even if it seems to have flown under the radar in the years since its release.

Just two weeks after the *Purple Rain* tour came to a close in Miami, Prince and the Revolution released their next album, *Around The World In A Day*. With a strong psychedelic approach, this was a big departure from that which came before it. The success *Purple Rain* brought Prince didn't diminish his core values or his constant search for perfection. Some felt he had found it with *Purple Rain*, but clearly, Prince didn't think the same. *Around The World In A Day* wasn't meant to be bigger and better than *Purple Rain*; it was simply meant to be different. Prince didn't do repetition, and it was clear from the 'Raspberry Beret' and 'Paisley Park' singles that there would be no repeat of 'Let's Go Crazy', 'When Doves Cry' or 'Purple Rain', and there didn't need to be. From the outside looking in, it seemed Prince was intentionally alienating himself from the new fan base he had only just been acquainted with, which attested to the struggles he experienced when trying to adjust to his heightened level of fame. In her 2018 interview with *The Guardian*, Lisa Coleman spoke of how Prince sought salvation inside his Paisley Park home, away from prying eyes. The glitz and glamour of cities like Los Angeles and New York wasn't for him:

> One of the reasons he stayed in Minnesota all his life is that it allowed him a little bit of freedom. It was hard after *Purple Rain* because it was limos and planes and thousands of people all the time. I think it was hard for him to decide when he could just be Prince, the guy, and when he had to become Prince, the superstar. He gave himself so thoroughly to it.

It was always going to be impossible to get away from *Purple Rain*, an album which has arguably carried Prince for most of his career, but the conscious performer was never not going to rise again. He did so with the huge hit 'Kiss', then with *Sign O' The Times* and Prince would go on to release 40-plus other albums, some of which have come since his passing.

For one reason or another, people know all the songs from *Purple Rain*, whether it be for the musical superfluities, the lyrical proclamations or the curious backstories which laid their foundations. Of all the songs though, it is the indelible title track which remains the most talked-about. Musically spellbinding and boasting what many critics consider to be one of the greatest guitar solos ever put to tape, 'Purple Rain' has almost as strong a legacy as its accompanying album, and it wasn't even a number-one hit.

In 1985, Prince reflected on how he was able to balance his roles as band leader and bandmate. Here, he speaks of his love for the members of The Revolution, whose own impacts on Prince's career and *Purple Rain* cannot ever be underestimated. Prince and the Revolution – a match made in musical heaven:

I strive for perfection, and I'm a little bullheaded in my ways. Then sometimes everybody in the band comes over, and we have very long talks. They're few and far between, and I do a lot of the talking. Whenever we're done, one of them will come up to me and say, 'Take care of yourself. You know I really love you'. I think they love me so much and I love them so much that if they came over all the time, I wouldn't be able to be to them what I am, and they wouldn't be able to do for me as what they do. I think we all need our individual spaces, and when we come together with what we've concocted in our heads, it's cool.

Bibliography

The following websites were used for research:

Americansongwriter.com

Billboard.com

Clashmusic.com

Faroutmagazine.co.uk

Genius.com

Goldiesparade.co.uk

Guitar.com

Housequake.com

Kerrang.com

Kottke.org

Loudersound.com

Mixdownmag.com.au

Nme.com

Paisleypark.com

Pitchfork.com

Popmatters.com

Prince.com

Prince.org

Princevault.com

Rollingstone.com

Smoothradio.com

Songfacts.com

Spin.com

Thecurrent.org

Theguardian.com

Thequietus.com

Thisisdig.com

On Track Series

Allman Brothers Band – Andrew Wild 978-1-78952-252-5
Tori Amos – Lisa Torem 978-1-78952-142-9
Aphex Twin – Beau Waddell 978-1-78952-267-9
Asia – Peter Braidis 978-1-78952-099-6
Badfinger – Robert Day-Webb 978-1-878952-176-4
Barclay James Harvest – Keith And Monica Domone
978-1-78952-067-5
Beck – Arthur Lizie 978-1-78952-258-7
The Beatles – Andrew Wild 978-1-78952-009-5
The Beatles Solo 1969-1980 – Andrew Wild 978-1-78952-030-9
Blue Oyster Cult – Jacob Holm-Lupo 978-1-78952-007-1
Blur – Matt Bishop 978-178952-164-1
Marc Bolan And T.rex – Peter Gallagher 978-1-78952-124-5
Kate Bush – Bill Thomas 978-1-78952-097-2
Camel – Hamish Kuzminski 978-1-78952-040-8
Captain Beefheart – Opher Goodwin 978-1-78952-235-8
Caravan – Andy Boot 978-1-78952-127-6
Cardiacs – Eric Benac 978-1-78952-131-3
Nick Cave And The Bad Seeds – Dominic Sanderson
978-1-78952-240-2
Eric Clapton Solo – Andrew Wild 978-1-78952-141-2
The Clash – Nick Assirati 978-1-78952-077-4
Elvis Costello And The Attractions – Georg Purvis 978-1-78952-129-0
Crosby, Stills And Nash – Andrew Wild 978-1-78952-039-2
Creedence Clearwater Revival – Tony Thompson 978-178952-237-2
The Damned – Morgan Brown 978-1-78952-136-8
Deep Purple And Rainbow 1968-79 – Steve Pilkington
978-1-78952-002-6
Dire Straits – Andrew Wild 978-1-78952-044-6
The Doors – Tony Thompson 978-1-78952-137-5
Dream Theater – Jordan Blum 978-1-78952-050-7
Eagles – John Van Der Kiste 978-1-78952-260-0
Earth, Wind And Fire – Bud Wilkins 978-1-78952-272-3
Electric Light Orchestra – Barry Delve 978-1-78952-152-8
Emerson Lake And Palmer – Mike Goode 978-1-78952-000-2
Fairport Convention – Kevan Furbank 978-1-78952-051-4
Peter Gabriel – Graeme Scarfe 978-1-78952-138-2
Genesis – Stuart Macfarlane 978-1-78952-005-7
Gentle Giant – Gary Steel 978-1-78952-058-3

Also Available From Sonicbond

Gong – Kevan Furbank 978-1-78952-082-8
Green Day – William E. Spevack 978-1-78952-261-7
Hall And Oates – Ian Abrahams 978-1-78952-167-2
Hawkwind – Duncan Harris 978-1-78952-052-1
Peter Hammill – Richard Rees Jones 978-1-78952-163-4
Roy Harper – Opher Goodwin 978-1-78952-130-6
Jimi Hendrix – Emma Stott 978-1-78952-175-7
The Hollies – Andrew Darlington 978-1-78952-159-7
Horslips – Richard James 978-1-78952-263-1
The Human League And The Sheffield Scene –
Andrew Darlington 978-1-78952-186-3
The Incredible String Band – Tim Moon 978-1-78952-107-8
Iron Maiden – Steve Pilkington 978-1-78952-061-3
Joe Jackson – Richard James 978-1-78952-189-4
Jefferson Airplane – Richard Butterworth 978-1-78952-143-6
Jethro Tull – Jordan Blum 978-1-78952-016-3
Elton John In The 1970s – Peter Kearns 978-1-78952-034-7
Billy Joel – Lisa Torem 978-1-78952-183-2
Judas Priest – John Tucker 978-1-78952-018-7
Kansas – Kevin Cummings 978-1-78952-057-6
The Kinks – Martin Hutchinson 978-1-78952-172-6
Korn – Matt Karpe 978-1-78952-153-5
Led Zeppelin – Steve Pilkington 978-1-78952-151-1
Level 42 – Matt Philips 978-1-78952-102-3
Little Feat – Georg Purvis - 978-1-78952-168-9
Aimee Mann – Jez Rowden 978-1-78952-036-1
Joni Mitchell – Peter Kearns 978-1-78952-081-1
The Moody Blues – Geoffrey Feakes 978-1-78952-042-2
Motorhead – Duncan Harris 978-1-78952-173-3
Nektar – Scott Meze – 978-1-78952-257-0
New Order – Dennis Remmer – 978-1-78952-249-5
Nightwish – Simon Mcmurdo – 978-1-78952-270-9
Laura Nyro – Philip Ward 978-1-78952-182-5
Mike Oldfield – Ryan Yard 978-1-78952-060-6
Opeth – Jordan Blum 978-1-78-952-166-5
Pearl Jam – Ben L. Connor 978-1-78952-188-7
Tom Petty – Richard James 978-1-78952-128-3
Pink Floyd – Richard Butterworth 978-1-78952-242-6
The Police – Pete Braidis 978-1-78952-158-0
Porcupine Tree – Nick Holmes 978-1-78952-144-3

Queen – Andrew Wild 978-1-78952-003-3
Radiohead – William Allen 978-1-78952-149-8
Rancid – Paul Matts 989-1-78952-187-0
Renaissance – David Detmer 978-1-78952-062-0
Reo Speedwagon – Jim Romag 978-1-78952-262-4
The Rolling Stones 1963-80 – Steve Pilkington 978-1-78952-017-0
The Smiths And Morrissey – Tommy Gunnarsson
978-1-78952-140-5
Spirit – Rev. Keith A. Gordon – 978-1-78952- 248-8
Stackridge – Alan Draper 978-1-78952-232-7
Status Quo The Frantic Four Years – Richard James
978-1-78952-160-3
Steely Dan – Jez Rowden 978-1-78952-043-9
Steve Hackett – Geoffrey Feakes 978-1-78952-098-9
Tears For Fears – Paul Clark - 978-178952-238-9
Thin Lizzy – Graeme Stroud 978-1-78952-064-4
Tool – Matt Karpe 978-1-78952-234-1
Toto – Jacob Holm-Lupo 978-1-78952-019-4
U2 – Eoghan Lyng 978-1-78952-078-1
Ufo – Richard James 978-1-78952-073-6
Van Der Graaf Generator – Dan Coffey 978-1-78952-031-6
Van Halen – Morgan Brown – 9781-78952-256-3
The Who – Geoffrey Feakes 978-1-78952-076-7
Roy Wood And The Move – James R Turner 978-1-78952-008-8
Yes – Stephen Lambe 978-1-78952-001-9
Frank Zappa 1966 To 1979 – Eric Benac 978-1-78952-033-0
Warren Zevon – Peter Gallagher 978-1-78952-170-2
10cc – Peter Kearns 978-1-78952-054-5

Decades Series

The Bee Gees In The 1960s – Andrew Mon Hughes Et Al
978-1-78952-148-1
The Bee Gees In The 1970s – Andrew Mon Hughes Et Al
978-1-78952-179-5
Black Sabbath In The 1970s – Chris Sutton 978-1-78952-171-9
Britpop – Peter Richard Adams And Matt Pooler 978-1-78952-169-6
Phil Collins In The 1980s – Andrew Wild 978-1-78952-185-6
Alice Cooper In The 1970s – Chris Sutton 978-1-78952-104-7
Alice Cooper In The 1980s – Chris Sutton 978-1-78952-259-4
Curved Air In The 1970s – Laura Shenton 978-1-78952-069-9

Donovan In The 1960s – Jeff Fitzgerald 978-1-78952-233-4
Bob Dylan In The 1980s – Don Klees 978-1-78952-157-3
Brian Eno In The 1970s – Gary Parsons 978-1-78952-239-6
Faith No More In The 1990s – Matt Karpe 978-1-78952-250-1
Fleetwood Mac In The 1970s – Andrew Wild 978-1-78952-105-4
Fleetwood Mac In The 1980s – Don Klees 978-178952-254-9
Focus In The 1970s – Stephen Lambe 978-1-78952-079-8
Free And Bad Company In The 1970s – John Van Der Kiste
978-1-78952-178-8
Genesis In The 1970s – Bill Thomas 978178952-146-7
George Harrison In The 1970s – Eoghan Lyng 978-1-78952-174-0
Kiss In The 1970s – Peter Gallagher 978-1-78952-246-4
Manfred Mann's Earth Band In The 1970s – John Van Der Kiste
978178952-243-3
Marillion In The 1980s – Nathaniel Webb 978-1-78952-065-1
Van Morrison In The 1970s – Peter Childs - 978-1-78952-241-9
Mott The Hoople And Ian Hunter In The 1970s –
John Van Der Kiste 978-1-78-952-162-7
Pink Floyd In The 1970s – Georg Purvis 978-1-78952-072-9
Suzi Quatro In The 1970s – Darren Johnson 978-1-78952-236-5
Queen In The 1970s – James Griffiths 978-1-78952-265-5
Roxy Music In The 1970s – Dave Thompson 978-1-78952-180-1
Slade In The 1970s – Darren Johnson 978-1-78952-268-6
Status Quo In The 1980s – Greg Harper 978-1-78952-244-0
Tangerine Dream In The 1970s – Stephen Palmer
978-1-78952-161-0
The Sweet In The 1970s – Darren Johnson 978-1-78952-139-9
Uriah Heep In The 1970s – Steve Pilkington 978-1-78952-103-0
Van Der Graaf Generator In The 1970s – Steve Pilkington
978-1-78952-245-7
Rick Wakeman In The 1970s – Geoffrey Feakes 978-1-78952-264-8
Yes In The 1980s – Stephen Lambe With David Watkinson
978-1-78952-125-2

On Screen Series
Carry On… – Stephen Lambe 978-1-78952-004-0
David Cronenberg – Patrick Chapman 978-1-78952-071-2
Doctor Who: The David Tennant Years – Jamie Hailstone
978-1-78952-066-8
James Bond – Andrew Wild 978-1-78952-010-1

Monty Python – Steve Pilkington 978-1-78952-047-7

Seinfeld Seasons 1 To 5 – Stephen Lambe 978-1-78952-012-5

Other Books

1967: A Year In Psychedelic Rock – Kevan Furbank
978-1-78952-155-9

1970: A Year In Rock – John Van Der Kiste 978-1-78952-147-4

1973: The Golden Year Of Progressive Rock – Geoffrey Feakes
978-1-78952-165-8

Babysitting A Band On The Rocks – G.D. Praetorius
978-1-78952-106-1

Eric Clapton Sessions – Andrew Wild 978-1-78952-177-1

Derek Taylor: For Your Radioactive Children –
Andrew Darlington 978-1-78952-038-5

The Golden Road: The Recording History Of The Grateful Dead –
John Kilbride 978-1-78952-156-6

Iggy And The Stooges On Stage 1967-1974 – Per Nilsen
978-1-78952-101-6

Jon Anderson And The Warriors – The Road To Yes –
David Watkinson 978-1-78952-059-0

Magic: The David Paton Story – David Paton 978-1-78952-266-2

Misty: The Music Of Johnny Mathis – Jakob Baekgaard
978-1-78952-247-1

Nu Metal: A Definitive Guide – Matt Karpe 978-1-78952-063-7

Tommy Bolin: In And Out Of Deep Purple – Laura Shenton
978-1-78952-070-5

Maximum Darkness – Deke Leonard 978-1-78952-048-4

The Twang Dynasty – Deke Leonard 978-1-78952-049-1

and many more to come!

Would you like to write for Sonicbond Publishing?

We are mainly a music publisher, but we also occasionally publish
in other genres including film and television. At Sonicbond
Publishing we are always on the look-out for authors, particularly
for our two main series, On Track and Decades.

Mixing fact with in depth analysis, the On Track series examines
the entire recorded work of a particular musical artist or group.
All genres are considered from easy listening and jazz to 60s
soul to 90s pop, via rock and metal.

The Decades series singles out a particular decade in an artist
or group's history and focuses on that decade in more detail
than may be allowed in the On Track series.

While professional writing experience would, of course, be
an advantage, the most important qualification is to have real
enthusiasm and knowledge of your subject. First-time authors are
welcomed, but the ability to write well in English is essential.

Sonicbond Publishing has distribution throughout Europe and
North America, and all our books are also published in E-book
form. Authors will be paid a royalty based on sales of their book.

Further details about our books are available from
www.sonicbondpublishing.com. To contact us, complete the
contact form there or email info@sonicbondpublishing.co.uk